Seeds for Sermons, Talks, and Addresses

Theme-Based Papers Written and
Compiled by Mary Hampton Battle

Edited and Submitted by her
daughter Edna Yvonne James

CROSSBOOKS
PUBLISHING

CrossBooks™
A Division of LifeWay
1663 Liberty Drive
Bloomington, IN 47403
www.crossbooks.com
Phone: 1-866-879-0502

First published by CrossBooks 1/28/2012

ISBN: 978-1-4627-1355-4 (hc)
ISBN: 978-1-4627-1356-1 (e)
ISBN: 978-1-4627-1357-8 (sc)

Library of Congress Control Number: 2012900599

Printed in the United States of America

This book is printed on acid-free paper.

Table of Contents

SEEDS FOR SERMONS, TALKS & ADDRESSES

Dedication

This book is dedicated to all of the officers and members of the now defunct New Zion District Association of the Illinois State Baptist Convention, Incorporated, whose lives touched and were touched by my mother, Mary Lee Hampton Battle (deceased), President Emeritus of the Women's Auxiliary. This book represents the decades that all worked together under Rev. James Macon, Moderator Emeritus and his wife, Sis. Joann Macon (deceased), First Vice-President of the Women's Auxiliary who not only shared in the leadership of New Zion District but were also best friends to my mom.

Preface

A sower went out to sow his seed [. . .] the seed is the word of God (Luke 8:5a, 11b). *Seeds for Sermons, Talks & Addresses* is a collection of talks and addresses given by and compiled by Mary Lee Hampton Battle. As President of the Women's Auxiliary of the New Zion District Association of the Illinois Baptist State Convention, Incorporated, Mary gave an annual accounting of the affairs of the district and accountability of her services rendered. She then proceeded to discuss the annual theme and theme scripture that had been selected for that year. Mary was president from 1974-1997, twenty-three years.

In addition to her President's Annual Address, she was often invited by churches to speak at various occasions, especially Women's Days, throughout the community. Mary carefully stored the handwritten papers in a large loose leaf, three ringed notebook in chronological order of the dates. Almost seven years after Mary's home going in September 2003, the notebook was discovered neatly shelved among her other books and Bibles; my sister had never disturbed her special storage closet.

Because the papers were written "by the aid of the Holy Spirit" as she so often stated and because she often said that if the speech did not line-up with the Bible, it was no good, I decided to prepare them for publication. In typing and editing the papers, I updated the scripture references by replacing "ye", "thee", "thy", and "thou" with "you" or "your" and sometimes eliminating them if the meaning was not destroyed or changed as well as updating words like "whither", "nigh," etc. Because Mary was so knowledgeable about the Scriptures through her personal studies and preparations as a Bible study teacher and a student at Brooks

Bible Institute, it was sometimes difficult to determine if she was making direct quotes or just paraphrasing since she used the Word in her daily conversation and was an outstanding Bible teacher. These were her personal papers so she did not have to name all of her resources though she named some. The bibliography is a listing of books that could be resources that were found in her closet. She also often cut out articles from newspapers to share with others. The Word of God was a part of her; she was saturated with the Word of God. Unless otherwise noted, she used *The Scofield Reference Bible.*

Since Mary used so many scriptures to back up the information in the papers and so many colorful metaphors, there were plenty of ideas or "seeds" for sermons for new or seasoned ministers and any others who need ideas for speaking occasions. Why she kept them all, I do not know, but the local Christian Book Store owner, Grace, said that it was to share with the world because there are so many people entering the ministry, and they need resources. With the exception of Perspective II, which I wrote when I was Youth President, one Women's Day paper, and a Women's Conference Outline which I included, these are Mary L. Hampton Battle's "seeds". Hopefully, these seeds will fall on good ground and spring up and bear fruit "an hundredfold" (Luke 8:8a).

Edna Y. James

LOOKING UNTO JESUS AND
WALKING WITH HIM

Psalm 1:1; Hebrews 12:2

Psalm 1:1 - *Blessed is the man who walks not in the counsel of the ungodly, nor stands in the way of sinners, nor sits in the seat of the scornful.*

Hebrews 12:2 - *Looking unto Jesus, the author and finisher of our faith, who for the joy that was set before Him endured the cross, despising the shame, and is set down at the right hand of the throne of God.*

In Psalm 1:1 we find out about two men, two ways, two destinies: the godly man and the ungodly man; there is a difference. In Scripture the number two is the number of division and separation. Exodus 8:23 tells us that God said, "I will put a division between my people and your people."

In Hebrews 12:2 we find out about one man, Jesus, with one way, "the same yesterday, and today, and forever;" and with one destiny, to be the author and finisher of our faith, to seal our faith. There is no difference; one stands alone. The number one is a primary number. Primary means first in rank, importance, or value. All other numbers depend upon number one. It precedes and produces all other numbers, meaning that every digit is dependent upon number one. So, in Scripture the number one is God's number; without Him (God) nothing could exist. "In the beginning God. . .," number one.

Now, take note that the psalmist's first word is "Blessed," a beatitude, like the sermon on the mountain. A lot of beatitudes are found in the psalms, but we will concentrate on Psalm1:1: "Blessed is the man who walks not in the counsel of the ungodly, nor stands in the way of sinners, nor sits in the seat of the scornful." This verse speaks about two men, the godly man and the ungodly man; there is a difference. In contrast the godly man is happy, Bible-centered, and prosperous; the ungodly man is unlike the godly man because he, the ungodly man, is doomed to judgment. Further down, in verse 3 it tells us, "And he (the godly man) shall be like a tree planted by the rivers of water, that brings forth its fruit in its season; its leaf also shall not wither; and whatsoever he does shall prosper." What is David, the psalmist, saying? If anybody should know, it's David, for he was a man after God's own heart (Acts 13:22). David knew that except the Lord does the building or planting, it's all in vain.

Lets kind of retrace our steps to see how we got to this point of contrast between the "planted" godly man and the *judged* ungodly man. In the beginning God created man in His image and likeness with the intention of man having fellowship with Him in obedience. Man's first home was in the Garden of Eden; God had planted a garden there. In the garden was every tree that is pleasant to the sight (not every kind) and good for food. There were two special trees in the midst of the garden: the tree of life and the tree of the knowledge of good and evil. It was here, in this garden, that God put (set or planted) the man, Adam.

Take note, trees in Scripture have important symbolical meanings. Notice the two trees in the garden: the tree of the choice of good and evil you can eat from it; that's your choice ("choose you this day whom you will serve" [Joshua 24:15], and then the tree of life, Number One's tree for only He, God, can give life since He is "the way, the truth, and the life" (John 1:6).

My friends, I'm trying to paint a picture. Like the artist who stands back and looks at what has been painted and then goes back to the picture to do some touch ups or highlighting and things like that, if I stop and look and touch up or highlight, I'm still trying to paint the picture. I'm trying to tell you and show you how this man Adam, the godly man was planted, by God, in the Garden of Eden by the rivers of water, the Pishon, Gihon, Hiddekel, and Euphrates. This godly man was happy, God-centered, and prosperous until along came the ungodly man, Satan, who was very unhappy. Satan knew that he was doomed to judgment because all he had been doing since God had kicked him out of heaven was "going to and fro and walking up and down in the earth." Here, he comes along and causes Adam to transgress the law of God by telling them ("male and female created he them" (Genesis 1:27) that they could have what God had kept for Himself.

Adam probably lamented as in Isaiah 6:5, "Woe is me, woe is me, I am undone, I am a man of unclean lips." I can hear him saying, "I was driven from my happy home, where there were beautiful trees, and herbs, and fruit which now has become a place of thistles, thorns, and briers. I now have to sweat and toil to make it. My wife will have pain in childbearing all because I became disobedient and greedy. You see, God had made me in His image and likeness; this means I had thinking, feelings and a will. I also was made up of body, soul, and spirit. I still have thinking, feeling, a will, body, and soul, but I lost the spirit. I forgot that I was made out of dust and that the spirit that God gave me will come back to Him who gave it (Ecclesiastes 12:7). What am I going to do now? What will happen to me? Things have reversed; God no longer comes into the garden to walk and talk with me. Now I have to go unto God and try to get whole again. Then I remembered when God had said in the Garden of Eden that one would come and make things right" (Gen.3:15), "the author and finisher of our faith."

My friends, this is the promise of the one man, the one way, the one destiny, the God man, not Mary's baby; a God Baby cannot do a Man's job. I'm talking about God, the Son, who had not yet become the God man. Wait a minute; before God the Father sent God the Son, He searched for a man, and He saw that there was no man and that there was no intercessor (Isaiah 59:16). So, the God Head got together and decided to make another Adam, for "The first man Adam was made a living soul; the last Adam was made a life giving spirit" (I Corinthians 15:45).

For this reason, when Christ was about to come into the world, He said to God, "You do not want sacrifices and offerings, but you have prepared a body for me. You are not pleased with animals burned whole on the altar or with sacrifices to take away sins. "Then I said, Here am I to do your will, O God just as it is written of me in the book of the law" (Hebrews:10:5-7), and so began the establishment, the authoring, the penning of our faith. The story, as written in Luke, began when God the Son, got on the train of nature, came down through 42 generations, got off in Bethlehem, but grew up in Nazareth. As was the custom, Jewish boys from the ages of 12, 13, and 14 have reached adulthood. At the age of 12, Mary's Baby, this God child, became the God man for He told His mother, "I must be about my Father's business" (Luke 2:49). His parents did not understand what He was talking about, but He was obedient to His earthly parents and "increased in wisdom and stature and in favor with God and man" (Lk. 2:50, 52).

Yes, my friends, Jesus was in the preparation period until the age of 30 then came upon the scene preaching, "Repent for the Kingdom of God is at hand." To establish our faith He taught many things and performed many miracles just as had been prophesied of old. In Isaiah 53:2, in the *Good News Bible*, "It was the will of the Lord that His servant grows like a plant taking root in dry ground." Ezekiel 34:29 says, "And I will raise up for them a plant of renown, and they shall be no more consumed with hunger in the land, neither bear the shame of the nations any more." "He shall be like a tree, planted [. . .], and brings forth fruit [. . .]."

Just as the first Psalm stated that a godly man would bear fruit, Jesus, the God man who became "the first born of many brothers" (Romans 8:29) came teaching the same thing. In John 15:1 Jesus declared, "I am the true vine," not a strange vine like Israel who was planted "a noble vine, wholly a right seed" (Jeremiah 2:21), but look what they became, a rotten, worthless vine. Jesus is that true vine, and, in His own words, "Every plant which my heavenly Father hath not planted, shall be rooted up" (Matthew 15:13).

Brothers and sisters, when we walk with the Lord, we will do as the Master has ordered, bear fruit. The Psalms begin with the benefits of being a godly, fruit bearing person, so why not bear fruit? The only way that we can bear fruit is through cleansing by being washed in Jesus' blood and the water of the word, through abiding in the True Vine, and obedience to our Heavenly Father. Then you will be able to do as our theme text in Hebrews 12:2, "Looking unto Jesus the author and finisher of our faith, who for the joy that was set before him endured the cross, despising the shame, and is set down at the right hand of God." Whom else can we look to? Go to the source, the author; the author writes the book with a beginning, middle, and an end. Jesus, our example, began establishing our faith from His birth, put in all of the middle during His life on earth, and finished our faith at the cross when He declared, "It is finished!"

Finally, I feel like the first man Adam messed up like we all do, but the second Man Adam, Jesus, the life giving Spirit, gave His life on the cross and proved that he finished the job when he was resurrected so all of us "Adams" can get right with God. The invitation is extended to you. Get right with God, and do it now. Open up your heart, and He will show you how. Look unto Jesus and walk with Him.

THERE IS A WAY

Isaiah 35:8-10

Isaiah 35:8-10: And an highway shall be there, and a way, and it shall be called The way of holiness; the unclean shall not pass over it, but it shall be for those: the wayfaring men, though fools, shall not err therein. No lion shall be there, nor any ravenous beast shall go up thereon; it shall not be found there, but the redeemed shall walk there. And the ransomed of the Lord shall return, and come to Zion with songs and everlasting joy upon their heads: they shall obtain joy and gladness, and sorrow and sighing shall flee away.

The writer of this scripture is Isaiah. His father's name was Amoz (1:1). He was married to a prophetess (8:3) and had two sons, Shear-jashub (7:3) and Maher-shalal-hash-baz (8:3). Their names were symbolic of the nation's history which Isaiah enforced in his prophecies. Shear-jashub means "a remnant shall return" (7:3) and Maher-shalal-hash-baz implies that riches and spoils shall be taken away (8:1-4). Isaiah's original call to service is unrecorded, but in chapter six we have his vision and commission. As a prophet of Judah, Isaiah ministered during the reign of Uzziah, Jotham, Ahab, and Hezekiah, kings of Judah. He comes before us as a man of many parts-- a gifted man called of God as the first and chief of Israel's prophets and poets. As a writer Isaiah wrote a history of the reign of Uzziah and Ahaz (II Chronicles 26:22; 32:32). No other Old Testament writer uses so many beautiful, vivid illustrations, poems, and so much figurative language as Isaiah. Sometimes he was stern in tone, yet he could also be tender and compassionate (15:15; 16:9). The book bearing his name is made up of sixty-six chapters and is like a miniature Bible which has sixty-six books. Aside from being a writer Isaiah was a statesman, reformer, prophet, teacher, dreamer and poet, architect and builder, and a theologian.

Our scripture says, "And a highway shall be there and a way, and it shall be called The way of holiness." It speaks of who will and who will not travel the highway and the way. It speaks about who will walk this highway and way and what will happen at the end of the journey. The questions that came to my mind were:

1. What was meant by this highway and a way?

2. How do we get on the highway and get to the way of holiness?

To answer question #1, a highway is a main, direct, public road. Way is a path or manner of life. For question #2, we get on the highway and into "a way" by the acquisition or acquiring of faith. One thing about faith is that when you get it, one thing leads to another and another and another. My friends, our scripture implies that some traveling will be going on by the very fact that a highway will be there. If we are going to be traveling, some preparations will have to be made. We have to determine where we are going, how we are going, the route to take, clothes to wear, and all of the other necessities that are needed to travel. This is true in our natural lives, and it is true in our spiritual lives.

Here we are talking about our spiritual lives; as such, I want you to know that we are going to the land of the ransomed and the redeemed. We are going to walk via way of the spiritual Route 66, the Bible, God's Holy Word. The whole armor of God are the clothes; the other essentials are truth, righteousness, peace, faith, salvation, the Word of God, and prayer (Ephesians 6:13-18). These tell us where we are going, how we're going, the route to take, the clothes to wear, and all of the other things needed to travel on the King's Highway. Even the late African-American singer Nat King Cole knew that if you wanted to get to an important place, you had to get on Route 66. He took "66" as far as California; we are going "66" all the way from earth to heaven.

We are travelers on a long journey, and sometimes on the road there are long stretches before you see a gas station or rest stop, but you continue on you way "speaking to yourselves in psalms and hymns and spiritual songs, singing and making melody in your heart to the Lord; Giving thanks always for all things unto God and the Father in the name of our Lord Jesus Christ" (Ephesians 5:19-20). You have to read your road map, the

Bible, God's Holy word, which is the Blueprint that God has given for the future. Pay close attention to the road signs and way markers. There are only two signs, the sign of the cross and the crown. There are numerous way markers. To name a few, there are the Ten Commandments, the 23rd Psalm, The Beatitudes, and The Lord's Prayer. Along with these Jeremiah 31:21 tells us, "Set up way marks, make them high heaps: set your heart toward the highway, even the way which you went." As you walk, Isaiah 30:21 tells us, "Your ears shall hear a word behind you, saying This is the way, walk you in it, when you turn to the right hand, and when you turn to the left."

As you travel you will see many things, some pleasant, some not so pleasant. This is because there are all kinds and types of people traveling. We have the classic, the casual, and the contemporary according to the age that you live in. If you lived in the classic age, you lived in the age that served as a standard of excellence. You saw Abraham, the father of many nations, Isaac, the son of Abraham and his wife Sarah in their old age, Jacob, who saw a ladder extending from earth to heaven, and Jesus, the Lamb of God slain from the foundation of the world.

If you lived and traveled in the casual age, you were in the age of the migrants, those who migrated or moved from place to place. The unlearned men, fishers, tent makers, tax collectors, and Jesus Christ all going out on Matthew Drive, Mark Street, and Luke, John, and Acts Lanes telling men, women, boys, and girls to repent for the Kingdom of God is at hand.

If you are living and traveling in the contemporary age, this is the now age, the present. You should get on the Roman Road telling everyone everywhere you go, "Brethren my hearts desire and prayer to God [for mine own people is that you are] saved" (Romans 10:1), for "All have sinned and come short of the glory of God" (Rom. 3:23), and that "the wages of sin is death; but the gift of God is eternal life" (Rom.6:23). Tell the Good News, the Gospel, which is about the death, burial, and the resurrection of our Lord and Savior Jesus Christ. Jesus lives in every age and even before this world began. Whatever your life style was or is you will have to choose who you are going to serve. One thing is for sure, everyone will not walk on this highway. No fools will walk on this highway. A fool is a person who does not believe in God, for the psalmist declared in Psalm14:1, "The fool has said in his heart there is no God." Since this is a restricted highway, there is no need to fear as we walk on the King's Highway; besides, God will be with us "always, even to the end of the world" (Matthew 28:20).

My friends, now that we know about the highway and how to get on it, let us go on to the part that says "and a way [. . .]." John 14:1-6 records a conversation Jesus has with His disciples, "Let not your heart be troubled: you believe in God, believe also in me. In my Father's house are many mansions; if it were not so, I would have told you. I go to prepare a place for you. And if I go and prepare a place for you, I will come again, and receive you unto myself, that where I am, there you may be also. And where I go you know, and the way you know. Thomas said unto Him, Lord we know not where you go; and how can we know the way? Jesus said unto him, I am the way, the truth, and the life; no man comes unto the Father, but by me." Jesus identifies Himself as the way, path, or manner of life that leads to holiness.

Jesus tells us in Matthew 7:13-14, "Enter in at the narrow gate; for wide is the gate, and broad is the way, that leads to destruction, and many there be who go in that way; Because narrow is the gate, and hard is the way which leads unto life, and few there be that find it." Luke 9:23 says, "If any man will come after me, let him deny himself, and take up his cross daily, and follow me." Jesus is able, now and always, to save those who come unto God through Him, and He lives forever to plead with God for you (Hebrews 7:25). We have Jesus' words and the record, that is for our benefit, that the way will not be easy, and in order to get to where we are going, we must follow Jesus.

So, when trouble like mountains get in the way let us have the same determination that Caleb had. After coming out of the wilderness to the land of promise, the children of Israel had to fight to get the inheritance. So Caleb, in the request for what he wanted, made this statement unto Joshua, "You know what the Lord said in Kadesh Barnea about you and me to Moses, the man of God. I was forty years old when the Lord's servant Moses sent me from Kadesh Barnea to spy out this land. I brought an honest report back to him. The men who went with me, however, made our people afraid. But I wholly followed the Lord my God. Because I did, Moses promised me that my children and I would certainly receive as our possession the land which I walked over. But now look. It has been forty-five years since the Lord said that to Moses. That was when Israel was going through the desert, and the Lord, as he promised has kept me alive ever since. Look at me! I am eighty-five years old and am just as strong today as I was when Moses sent me out. I am still strong enough for war or anything else. Now, therefore, give me this mountain that the Lord promised me on that day when the men reported" (Joshua 14:6-12).

Brothers and sisters, God is telling us through this passage of scripture in "66", the route and way we are traveling, that regardless of how old you may get to be, He is your "refuge and strength, a very present help in trouble" (Psalm 46:1). "It is He that has made us and not we ourselves" (Psalm 100:3); it is through Him that "we live and move, and have our being" (Acts 17:28), and His yoke is easy and His burden is light (Matthew 11:30).

Yes, my friends, if you read and study our blueprint which is the Bible, travel via "66", and follow the directions; you will live in total bliss forever and ever. If you don't, it's because you failed to get on "66". Yes, "There Is A Way." It's an appointed way, a highway, a holy way, a plainly marked way, a safe way where the redeemed will return joyfully to Zion with everlasting exultation at last obtaining "happiness, with sorrow and sighing fleeing away" (Isaiah 35:10). Thank you.

CALLED TO SERVE

Ephesians 2:10

Ephesians 2:10 - For we are God's workmanship created in Christ Jesus to do good works, which God prepared in advance for us to do.

One definition of the word "called" means to announce in a loud voice. The word "serve" means to obey, minister, or assist. To explore this topic I was led by the Spirit of God to the first chapter of the book of Genesis, the beginning. "In the beginning God created the heaven and the earth. And the earth was without form, and void; and darkness was upon the face of the deep. And the Spirit of God moved upon the face of the waters. And God said, Let there be [. . .]." This was the creative process of speaking things into existence until the sixth day. On the sixth day after the earth brought forth the living creatures after its kind, God saw that it was good. Notice, if you please, after everything that God made, He checked it out. Then, it passed inspection; it was good. So, on the sixth day after God finished all of the other creations, "God said, Let us make man in our image after our likeness; and let them have dominion over the fish of the sea, and over the fowl of the air, and over the cattle, and over all the earth, and over every creeping thing that creeps upon the earth. So, God created man in His own image, in the image of God created He him; male and female created He them" (vs. 26-27).

After God made man, God then prepared Eden for him. "And out of the ground made the Lord God to grow every tree that is pleasant to the sight, and good for food, the tree of life, and the tree of knowledge of good and evil were there" (2:8-9). Adam didn't have to worry about watering the garden because a river went through Eden. When all preparations had been made and finished, "God took the man, and put him into the garden to till it and to keep it" (2:15).

Then God made a bargain or covenant between Himself and Adam. Now, *Webster's Seventh New Collegiate Dictionary* defines bargain as an agreement between parties settling what each gives or receives in a transaction between them or what course of action or policy each pursues in respect to the other. We find in the record in Genesis 2:8-17 where Adam was to dress the garden, or, as we would say, keep the trees and shrubs pruned. This was his only obligation to God for allowing him to live in Eden. In return for dressing and keeping the garden, Adam was to eat of all the fruit of the garden - - except from one tree. Adam accepted, and what a bargain he received!

Now let us look at the definition of a bargain again: to agree on terms; an agreement between parties; a contract regarding terms. Certainly there was an agreement between God and Adam. Adam could have turned down God's proposition. This is proven by the fact that he later ignored God's warning concerning the forbidden fruit. Adam was not a puppet on a string; he was a human being made in the image of God. He had a will and a mind, and he used his own will when he ate the forbidden fruit. Therefore, it stands to reason that since Adam had a free will, at the beginning Adam could have turned down God's proposition to live in the Garden of Eden, dress it, keep it, and eat the fruit of it; however, he accepted.

After Adam accepted God's offer, "The Lord God caused a deep sleep to fall upon Adam; and [God] took one of Adam's ribs, and closed up the flesh. And the rib which God had taken from Adam, made He a woman, and brought her unto the man" (2:21-22). This is when the first marriage took place. For the Scripture declares, "Therefore shall a man leave his father and mother, and shall cleave unto his wife: and they shall be one flesh" (2:24). What a bargain Adam had! Adam and all the creation, plants, and animals were made for God's glory, honor, and purpose and to serve Him. Even though Adam had sovereignty over the earth, he was to have fellowship with God and still be subject to God, his creator. Although the plants, animals, and other living creatures were for man's purpose, yet these, too, are subject to God, their creator.

My friends, Adam and Eve lived in peace and harmony with God to serve His purpose, and every day in the cool of the day God visited them. Why not, for you see Adam was God's earthly son (Luke 3:38), God's earthly family, and as a father, God provided for His family. I Timothy 5:8 teaches us, "But if any provide not for his own house (or family), he has denied the faith, and is worse than an infidel." I don't know how long Adam and Eve lived in the Garden of Eden before they were put out for breaking the agreement, but even after the break up of the family, God the Father still provided for His earthly son Adam by the promise of a heavenly Son, Jesus, the last Adam. Genesis 3:15 tells us, "And I will put enmity between you and the woman and between your seed and her seed; he shall bruise your head and you shall bruise his heel."

Yes, when sin came, it caused a separation between God and man. Man lost sovereignty over the earth. Man was in enmity with God, and nature was in enmity with man. Now, the goal of God is to restore sinning man to God's likeness, fellowship, and dominion (Hebrews 2:8-10; Romans 8:17-19), then we will be prepared to "serve". Even though man has failed every test that God has given, the task is still the same, "Called to Serve".

So, in accordance with Genesis 3:15, we wait with patient assurance for God's complete victory on the earth (Romans 8:19-25). In order to prepare us to serve, God's promise of a seed had to be fulfilled. Isaiah prophesied, "For unto us a child is born, unto us a son is given, and the government shall be upon his shoulder; and his name shall be called wonderful, counselor, the mighty God, the Everlasting Father, the Prince of Peace" (Isa. 9:46). Forty-two generations after the promise was given, the promise came true. The mighty God, the Everlasting Father, took a part of Himself and wrapped it in dirt to look like us. He came through a virgin named Mary in order to reconcile us back to the family.

Now, you don't have to believe me; I didn't write the words. In John 8:42 Jesus Himself said, "For I proceeded forth and came from God; neither came I of myself, but he sent me." So God Himself came down to restore man back to Himself. It is often said that if you want something done right, you have to do it yourself. Of course, God is the only one able to meet the strenuous requirements. Scripture teaches, "Wherefore by one man sin entered into the world, and death by sin; and so death passed upon all men, for that all have sinned" (Romans 5:12). Therefore, "As by the offence of one, judgment came upon all men to condemnation; even so by the righteousness of one the free Gift came upon all men unto justification of life. For as by one man's disobedience many were made sinners, so by the obedience of one (Jesus) shall many be made righteousness" (Romans 5:18-19).

Yes, my brothers and my sisters, many of us have been "called to serve". The call went out as a loud voice saying, "For by grace are you saved through faith; and that not of yourselves; it is the gift of God - - not of works, lest any man should boast. For we are his workmanship created in Christ Jesus to do good works, which God prepared in advance for us to do" (Ephesians 2:8-10); so, yes, we are "called to serve", "to do good works." Not only are we "called" to serve some are also "chosen" by God to serve. The Scripture teaches us, "Many are called but few chosen" (Matthew 22:14). "And he gave some, apostles; and some, prophets; and some evangelists; and some pastors and teachers; For the perfecting of the saints, for the work of the ministry, for the edifying of the body of Christ" (Ephesians 4:11-12). However, God calls all Christians to take certain actions regardless of age, experience, knowledge, or gifts. II Peter 1:10 tells us in the *Good News Bible* , "So then my brothers, try even harder to make God's call and His choice of you a permanent experience, if you do so, you will never abandon your faith."

My friends, God calls us to glorify Him, to honor Him, to serve Him, to serve others, and to invest our lives wisely. To glorify God everything we do should bring honor to Him and nothing should bring dishonor to His name. Colossians 3:23-24 tells us, "And whatever you do, do it heartily, as to the Lord, and not unto men knowing that of the Lord you shall receive the reward of the inheritance; for you serve the Lord Christ."

To honor God means keeping Christ first and involving Him in every aspect of our lives. Matthew 6:33-34 tells us, "But seek you first the Kingdom of God and His righteousness, and all these things shall be added unto you. Be, therefore, not anxious about tomorrow for tomorrow will be anxious for the things of itself. Sufficient unto the day is its own evil."

We also find that in order to serve God, we serve others. According to Luke 9:24, the person who loses his or her life will find it. So, instead of looking out for "number one", yourself, all the time, we should be looking out for others. When asked, "What is the great commandment?" Jesus Himself says, "You shall love the Lord your God with all your heart, and with all your soul, and with all your mind. This is the first and great commandment; and the second is like unto it, you shall love your neighbor as yourself. On these two commandments hang all the law and the prophets" (Matthew 22:37-40).

We should also invest our lives wisely. The parable of the talents found in Matthew 25:14-30 tells us that our attitudes should be that all we have is on loan from God and should be used and invested well. Just as a familiar slogan says "a mind is a terrible thing to waste," so a life is a terrible thing to waste. We, the saved, "have been called unto liberty; only use not liberty for an occasion to the flesh, but by love serve one another" (Galatians 5:13). Be reminded that you will give an account of your life. Our greatest example of serving is Jesus who came not to be served but to serve. Matthew 20:28 says, "Even as the Son of man came not to be ministered unto, but to minister, and to give His life a ransom for many." Galatians 6:10 tells us, "As we have opportunity, let us do good unto all men, especially unto them who are of the household of faith." We, like Christ, have been "Called to Serve."

FROM YONDER TO HERE

Psalm 37:25

Psalm 37:25 - I have been young and now am old; yet have I not seen the righteous forsaken, nor his seed begging bread.

The 37th Psalm was written by David. He was born in Bethlehem which was also called the City of David. He was the eighth son of Jesse. The number eight in Scripture means resurrection or a new beginning. David's name in Hebrew means beloved. In his youthful days David had extensive preparation, for during this time he learned how to play musical instruments, to fight off lions and bears, and to put his trust in God for divine aid. On one occasion, when he was on an errand of serving his older brothers who were in the army, David heard the giant Goliath challenging the Israelites. David let the people know that he would fight against Goliath, for he trusted in the Lord to deliver him out of Goliath's hands. You know the story as recorded in I Samuel, Chapter 17. Because of David's trust in God, God blessed him mightily during his career as a shepherd boy, a servant in the royal court, musician, psalmist, a fugitive of Israel, statesman, religious leader, and finally as the architect King and builder of Israel's empire.

The 37th Psalm is a sermon written by David, not for a devotional psalm or a praise psalm but a psalm of instruction and teaching. The psalmist starts the sermon with the statement, "Fret not yourself because of evil doers." David goes on in his sermon stating his philosophy of how to live in the midst of wicked people. His philosophy was to do good, trust God, and don't worry. Yes, from the Holy Scriptures we learned that David lived by his philosophy, for Scripture teaches us that David was "a man after God's own heart" (Acts 13:22). Skeptics will ask, "How can this be seeing as how he indulged in the sin of adultery and was also a murderer?" Well, my friends, David could not and did not escape the judgments of God, but when David acknowledged his iniquity as a penitent sinner, he qualified as a man who pleased God (I Samuel 13:14). You see, "Man looks on the outward appearance, but God looks on the heart (16:7). More than that, David never failed to recognize the fact that it was from God that all blessings flow, and God even made an everlasting covenant with David which stands today because of his lineage to Jesus.

"Yonder to Here," what a curious theme. My curiosity led me to the dictionary which defined the word "yonder" to mean within sight, but not near. The word "here" was described as in place; this life; the present. Our theme scripture says, "I have been young and now am old; yet have I not seen the righteous forsaken, nor his seed begging bread." This sermon is coming from a speaker with the voice of experience and wisdom, for David had lived long enough to know that "The earth is the Lord's and the fullness thereof; the world and they that dwell therein" (Psalm 24:1). He knew that the Lord was his divine Shepherd, and that "God is our refuge and strength, a very present help in trouble" (46:1). David relied completely upon God for all of his help, for he knew that all of his help came from God, whatever kind of help he needed. And, when he got old, he still maintained in the 71st Psalm, verse 1, "In you, O Lord, do I put my trust; let me never be put to confusion." David goes on in verses 5 and 6, "For you are my trust from my youth. By you have I been held up from the womb; you are he who took me out of my mother; my praise shall be continually of you." Verse 9 continues with, "Cast me not off in the time of old age; forsake me not when my strength fails."

Yes, my brothers and sisters, David, all of the Biblical characters who believed in God , and believers of a certain age today can look back on the "yonder" years of youth, the years that are in sight through our vivid memory but not near because we can never return, yet never forget, and say, "Look where he brought me from." We know that to get from "yonder to here" required faith then and still requires faith today, here and now. Ephesians 2:8 tells us, "For by grace are you saved through faith; and that not of yourselves; it is the gift of God." Scripture lets all mankind know that we are powerless without faith. In Matthew 17:14-21 we find the story about the man who had a dumb spirit. The Disciples could not cast the spirit out, but Jesus did. When the disciples asked Jesus why they could not cast out the dumb spirit, Jesus said it was because of their unbelief; "For verily I say unto you, If you have faith as a grain of mustard seed, you shall say unto this mountain move from *here to yonder* place; and it shall move; and nothing shall be impossible unto you," even from *yonder to here*!

Jesus compares our faith to a grain of mustard seed which must be planted near the surface in rich, fertile ground in order to flourish. As soon as a tiny shoot emerges, it must immediately obtain food and strength from another source. The same is true with our faith. Because our faith is so weak, it must reach beyond itself for sustenance and growth; "Your faith should not be in the wisdom of men, but in the power of God" (I Corinthians 2:5). Believers of a certain age with the "From Yonder to Here" experience should know this and be strong in the faith, so with our experiences behind us, what can we say to our young people who can only look ahead?

To the young people I say, "Remember now your creator in the days of your youth, while the evil days come not, nor the years draw near when you shall say, I have no pleasure in them" (Ecclesiastes 12:1). "Trust in the Lord with all your heart, and lean not unto your own understanding. In all your ways acknowledge him, and he shall direct your paths" (Proverbs 3:5-6). "Enter not into the path of the wicked and go not in the way of evil men; avoid it, pass not by it, turn from it, and pass away"(4:14-5). Young people don't get burdened down with what people call peer pressure. You don't have to join the Crypts or the Bloods gangs to belong. The only blood that you need is your own blood and the blood of Jesus. You don't have to hook up with a gang; you can hook up with Jesus and join a church. Your social organization, N.A.A.C.P. can be called the National Association for the Advancement of **Christian** people. This organization which works under the auspices of the new K.K.K., my **K**night, my **K**insman, my **K**ing, was organized by God in eternity past, goes through eternity future, and has more power than any gang. We exhort you, as given in *The Good News Bible,* to "Build up your strength in union with the Lord and by means of His mighty power. Put on all the armor that God gives you, so that you will be able to stand up against the wicked spiritual forces in the heavenly world, the rulers, authorities, and cosmic powers of these dark times. So put on God's armor now! Then when the evil day comes, you will be able to resist the enemy's attacks; and after fighting to the end, you will still hold your ground. So stand ready, with truth as a belt tight around your waist, with righteousness as your breastplate, and, as your shoes, the readiness to announce the good news of peace. At all times carry faith as a shield, for with it you will be able to put out all the burning arrows shot by the Evil One, accept salvation as a helmet, and the word of God as the sword which the Spirit gives you. Do all this in prayer while asking for God's help. Pray on every occasion as the Spirit leads. For this reason keep alert and never give up; pray always for all of God's people" (Ephesians 6:10-18). And Jesus also promises, "Lo, I will be with you always, even, to the end of the world" (Matthew 28:20).

Young people, another daily Pledge of Allegiance can be said: "I pledge allegiance to our God, the God of Abraham, Isaac, and Jacob, and to the republic for which He (God) stands; one nation, the saved, under God, with liberty, justice, and a heaven for all who believe on His name." And, always have your walkie-talkie in readiness. Some older saints got a telephone in their bosom; that might have worked then, but they might have been on a party line. These days you can be on three-way, but you run the risk of being put on hold. A cell phone and text messaging might be alright for some, but notice emergency situations require walkie-talkies because it is always in tune to the correct frequency for a direct line immediately. All you have to say is, "Come in." You can always be in communion with God who is the quality that breeds success.

Do all the good you can in all the ways you can for all the people you can while you can because to make a success of old age, you have to start young. Plan your life according to the word of God. If you fail to plan, then you plan to fail. If you do not want the fruits of sin, stay out of the devil's orchard. The Scriptures lets us know that though God formed us; sin deformed us; but Christ transforms us so we can get from here to yonder, the present to the future, and so we can finish our course. The same requirements that got us from "Yonder to Here" can be used to take all of us forward, both young and old.

We must "Hold fast to the profession of our faith without wavering" (Hebrews 10:23); we must persevere. "For it is God who works in you both to will and to do of His good pleasure"(Philippians 2:13). Finally, I leave you with a lesson on the rewards of perseverance. There is a story about two frogs that fell into a deep bowl of cream. The one was wise and a cheery soul. The other one took a gloomy view and bade his friend a sad,

"Adieu." Said the other frog with a merry grin, "I can't get out, but I won't give in; I'll swim around 'til my strength is spent, then I will die the more content." As he swam, though ever it seemed, his struggling began to churn the cream until on top of pure butter he stopped, and out of the bowl he quickly hopped. "What is the moral?" You ask. Oh, it's easily found! If you can't get out, keep swimming around.

PRESSING TOWARD THE MARK;
GOD HAS A JOB FOR YOU

Philippians 3:14

Philippians 3:14 - I press toward the mark for the prize of the high calling of God in Christ Jesus.

The writer of our scripture is Paul. This letter to the Philippians was written while Paul was in prison at Rome. The theme is "Joy in Christ". The key verse is "For me to live is Christ and to die is gain" (1:21). My thoughts fell on the subject: "God Has a Job for You."

There is no life of a higher quality in Christ than the life of the apostle Paul. His story is well known to most of us. When we examine the life of Paul before he experienced a radical change, we are reminded of his Pharisian zeal in the undertaking and execution of the law. By his own admission Saul of Tarsus, as he had been known, was fiercely devoted to his Jewish past as well as his Pharisian upbringing. He states in *The English Version* of Philippians 3:3b-6, "We do not put any trust in external ceremonies. I could, of course, put my trust in such things. If anyone thinks he can trust in external ceremonies, I have even more reason to feel that way. I was circumcised when I was eight days old. I am an Israelite by birth, of the tribe of Benjamin, a pure blooded Hebrew. As far as keeping the Jewish Law is concerned, I was a Pharisee, and I was so zealous that I persecuted the church. As far as a person can be righteous by obeying the commands of the Law, I was without fault."

Paul's admission of his fanatical loyalty to Judaism is a testimony to our human fidelities (faith, loyalty, devotion). All of us have alliances and allegiances to people, institutions, and things. However, when Christ comes into our lives, all alliances and allegiances dim because Christ is now in control, and He becomes pre-eminent in our lives. This is what happened to Saul of Tarsus on the Damascus Road as recorded in Acts 9:1-9. While on his journey to the city, a wonderful conversion took place radically changing, converting and transforming proud and persecuting Saul from an <u>under</u>taker to an <u>upper</u> taker. The conflict of Saul's feelings was so great and his remorse was so deep that during a period of three days he neither did eat nor drink. He could have no communication with the Christians for they had been terrified by the news of his approach, and the unconverted Jews had no sympathy with his present state of mind. But he called upon God, and in his blindness a vision was granted him -- a vision soon to be realized -- of his being restored to sight by Ananias. After his restoration he was baptized, communed with the disciples, and "straightway preached Christ in the synagogues, that He (Christ) is the Son of God" (Acts 9:20).

Because of this life changing experience, Paul declared in II Corinthians 5:17, "Therefore if any man be in Christ, he is a new creature; old things are passed away; behold all things are become new." Yes, Paul had a job to do. He knew how he got the job, when he got the job, and how to do the job. Galatians 1:11-18 says, in the *English Version Bible,* "Let me tell you, my brothers, that the gospel I preach is not of human origin. I did not receive it from any man, nor did anyone teach it to me. It was Jesus Christ himself who revealed it to me. You have been told how I used to live when I was devoted to the Jewish religion, how I persecuted without mercy the church of God and did my best to destroy it. I was ahead of most fellow Jews of my age in my practice of the Jewish religion, and was much more devoted to the tradition of our ancestors, But God in His grace chose me even before I was born, and called me to serve Him, and when He decided to reveal His Son to me, so that I might preach the Good News about Him to the Gentiles, I did not go to anyone for advice, nor did I go to Jerusalem to see those who were apostles before me. Instead, I went at once to Arabia, And then I returned to Damascus. It was three years later that I went to Jerusalem to obtain information from Peter, and I stayed with him for two weeks. I did not see any other apostle except James, the Lord's brother."

My brothers and sisters, just as Paul had a job to do, we have a job to do, and in the field of employment, secular or spiritual, there are certain requirements that must be met in order to get a job, skilled or unskilled:

- First we have to **prepare**, second, to **participate**, and third, **to persevere**.
- Then, we have to **want to**: that means prepare; that takes *faith*.
- We have to **go to**: that means participate; that takes *hope*.
- We also have to **keep to**: that means to persevere; that takes *love*.

The same requirements it takes to get the job are required to keep the job. Christ Himself had a job to do. Preparation had to be made. It started in the Garden of Eden when God told the serpent, "Because you have done this, you are cursed above all cattle, and above every beast of the field; upon your belly shall you go, and dust shall you eat all the days of your life. And I will put enmity between you and the woman,. And between your seed and her seed; he shall bruise your head, and you shall bruise his heel" (Genesis 3:14-15).

Well, it didn't take long for the prophecy to come true as far as the serpent was concerned. The first dust he ate was that of Abel whom God had recently formed out of the dust. He has been eating dust ever since; in fact, he is so prosperous that he formed a company. Did you know that Satan has one of the largest wrecking companies in the world? The company's name is L. S. D. & Company: Lucifer (his given name), Satan (his acquired name), Devil (what he is), & Company (a host of demons); no wonder LSD is a popular drug.

But, brothers and sisters, in spite of the L.S.D. & Company, we don't have to have any fear because the C.E.O is in charge: the Chief Executive Officer, God. God had made preparation for man's salvation. I don't believe God wanted to sacrifice His only begotten Son, you know how we are about our children. But, God looked through forty-two generations and could find no one. The Son Himself decided to come into the world. Hebrews 10:4-5, 7 says, "For it is not possible that the blood of bulls and of goats should take away sins. Wherefore, when he came into the world, he said, Sacrifice and offering you would not, but a body have you prepared me [. . .] Then said I, Lo I come in the volume of the book it is written of me to do your will, O God."

Yes, my friends, Jesus had a job to do; he was fully prepared. He came into the world full of grace and truth, and at the age of twelve declared to a dying world, "I must be about my Father's business" (Luke 2:49). Just as Jesus finished His work on earth and has ascended back to heaven, we, too, must be about the business of telling dying men, sinking women, girls, and boys that the wages of sin is death and the gift of God is eternal life. "Let us not forsake the assembling of ourselves together as some have; for we see the end fast approaching"(Hebrews 10:25). We are told to "Hold fast the profession of our faith without wavering, for God is faithful" (10:23).

My sisters and brothers, I know that God has a job for me to do. It took me a long time for my eyes to open and see all of the mistakes that I was making, but through all of my ups and downs the Lord finally revealed to me that the problem was Satan. You see, for a long time I didn't know about Satan and his wiles. My parents had taught me if I didn't get religion I would go to hell with the devil and that hell was hot. That's about all I knew about Satan. Well, I did learn how to lean and depend on Jesus. As I studied and learned more and more about Jesus, I found out that I didn't have to do what Satan put in my mind. I found out that Satan can put things on your mind, but he is not a mind reader; he does not know your mind until you voice it. He is not omnipotent, omniscient or omnipresent; only God is all of these things, hallelujah! For this cause I work for the Master. I know that living for Christ is high in benefits. There are some side effects, and that's what Satan dwells on and throws up in your face, but the abundant benefits far outweigh the minor side effects.

"Wherefore my friends, seeing we have this large crowd of witnesses around us (such as Abel, Enoch, Noah, Abraham and Sarah, Isaac, Jacob, Joseph, Moses, Joshua and Israel, Rahab and many, many more heroes of faith), let us rid ourselves of everything that gets in the way, and of the sin which holds on to us so tightly, and let us run with determination the race that lies before us. Let us keep our eyes fixed on Jesus on whom our faith depends from beginning to end. He did not give up because of the cross; on the contrary, because of the joy that was waiting for him, he thought nothing of the disgrace of dying on the cross, and he is now seated at the right side of God's throne" (Heb. 12:1-2).

This is what Paul was telling us when he stated, "I press toward the mark for the prize of the high calling of God in Christ." Paul had been caught up into Paradise, up to the third heaven where Jesus is. Like Moses, he, too, had gotten a glimpse of the Promised Land, and he knew what he would gain. He knew it so well that he stated, "For me to live is Christ and to die is gain" (Philippians 1:21). He, like us, had heard of the land of an unclouded day, but now he knew for certain.

I, myself, am going to work on my job until the Kingdom comes. "For thine is the Kingdom and the power and the glory forever" (Matthew 6:13). Brothers and sisters, God has a job for you, Amen.

WORKING FOR THE MASTER: YOU CAN DEPEND ON GOD FOR HE'S THE MASTER BUILDER

Nehemiah 4:6

Nehemiah 4:6 *- So built we the wall, and all the wall was joined together to half of its height; for the people had a mind to work.*

This scripture is taken from the Book of Nehemiah, which is also the name of the writer. The name means the Lord comforts. The Book of Nehemiah is in the History Division of the Old Testament. It is the eleventh book of history and the 16th book of the Old Testament. The main character is Nehemiah whom I greatly admire as a man of prayer, for it is recorded eleven times in the Book of Nehemiah that he engaged in prayer to God.

As I reflect back on Nehemiah and all of the good that he did for the people by the help of God, I thought about another great man, Rev. Dr. Martin Luther King, Jr., who used the words of a song to make this proclamation: "If I can help somebody as I pass along . . . If I can do my duty as a Christian ought, If I can bring salvation to a world once wrought . . . Then my living shall not be in vain."

Nehemiah was just such a man as this, doing all the good he could while he could. He was not just concerned about himself alone. He could have gone on and said, "I'm doing alright for myself. I've got a good job; I'm the king's cup bearer," but not so. If we read the entire Book of Nehemiah, we will find in Chapter 1 Nehemiah's inquiries about the Jews who were left -- of their captivity, of their affliction and reproach, and how the wall of Jerusalem was broken down, and its gates were burned with fire. Verse 4 of Chapter 1 says, "And it came to pass when I heard these words, that I sat down and wept, and mourned certain days and fasted, and prayed before the God of heaven." Not only did Nehemiah pray, the prayer was answered; God granted the petition that Nehemiah had placed before Him.

After praying and getting an answer, Nehemiah went to Jerusalem and encouraged the brethren to build the wall. You see, Nehemiah knew it was alright to build the wall because he had gotten the "Okie Dokie" from the Lord. I am sure he also knew that "Except the Lord build the house, they labor in vain that build it; except the Lord keep the city, the watchman wakes in vain" (Psalm 127:1). This wasn't all that Nehemiah did. In Chapter 4 we find his resistance to the enemy. In Chapter 5 he rebukes the brothers for their greed. In Chapter 6 we read about his faith and courage and his message, "I am doing a great work, so that I cannot come down. Why should the work cease?" In Chapter 8 he comforts the people; in Chapter 10 he seals (approves) the covenant; and in Chapter 13 he purifies the temple (vs. 1), punishes Sabbath breakers (vs. 15), annuls unlawful marriages (vs. 23), and ends by asking God to "remember me."

We can see from Nehemiah's life his complete dependence upon God to help him in all of his endeavors. It brings to mind the subject: "You Can Depend on God, For He's the Master Builder." The *World Book Dictionary* describes the phrase master builder as "a person skilled in planning and directing the construction of buildings." We also call master builders architects and contractors. In Ecclesiastes 3:1, 3 we find, "To everything there is a season and a time to every purpose under the heaven [. . .] a time to break down, and a time to build up." Genesis 1:1 says, "In the beginning God created the heaven and the earth. And the earth was without form and void; and darkness was upon the face of the deep. And the Spirit of God moved upon the face of the waters." John 1:3 says, "All things were made by him; and without him was not anything made that was made." This includes the world, man, things visible, and things invisible.

Isn't it sweet just to know that we, by faith, are under the jurisdiction of the person that made the whole world, the one who said, "Let there be [. . .]," knowing that it would *be.* In Isaiah 55:11 God said, "So shall my word be that go forth out of my mouth; it shall not return unto me void, but it shall accomplish that which I please, and it shall prosper in the thing whereto I sent it." Let us take a stroll down Time Square. As we walk along, let us take a panoramic view of the world. It has already been established that Elohim (English form of God) created and made the universe, and man was given dominion (rule) over it.

As we stroll down the avenue, we trip and *fall*; in the *fall* we sustain injuries. As we arise from the fall, we find that we have been **wounded for transgressions and bruised for iniquities.** As a result of the fall, we are forced into hard labor. The bruise festered into an open sore that bred murders, idolatry, corruption, and every imagination of the thoughts of our heart was only evil continually, and finally, death. But, wait, as we stroll I see Jehovah-jireh (the Lord will provide) making provisions for fallen humanity. God tells the "tripster", the serpent, "Because you have done this, you are cursed above all cattle and above every beast of the fields: upon your belly shall you go, and dust shall you eat all the days of your life. And I will put enmity between you and the woman, and between your seed and her seed, he shall bruise your head, and you shall bruise his heel" (Genesis 3:14-15).

As we continue to stroll down Time Square, we see the Master Builder getting tired of man whom He had created and made. He was so grieved in His heart that He decided, "I will destroy man whom I have created from the face of the earth, both man, beast, creeping things, and fowls of the air" (Gen. 6:7), all but my servant Noah and his family.

So, we continue in time on "Noah Boulevard" where the Noah family live. In passing by we can hear The Master Builder and Planner giving Mr. Noah the dimensions, style, and the type of material to use in the building of a huge boat. Many days later, just as it was in the beginning, the Spirit of God moved upon the face of the waters. Months passed, the waters have subsided, and this time, again, God will have to build the wasted places. As The Master Builder, He is the only one who can build up what has been torn down. Isaiah 61:14 says, "And they shall build the old wastes; they shall build up the former desolations, and they shall repair the waste cities, the desolation of many generations."

Yes, my friends, many centuries have passed since we started to stroll down Time Square. Now we find that we are moving into another time zone, and we have no time to lose. You see, The Master Builder got the news the other day that it's time to go down and build up that what has been torn down. So, Jesus, The Master Builder, the one who was in the beginning, the one who without Him was not anything made that was made, planned to come down and check things out. Jesus decided, "I can't go as I am because I'm invisible, so a body have you prepared me (Hebrews 10:5). I came down through 42 generations. I rode the time train of nature nine months; I got off in the City of David called Bethlehem. I was brought up by loving earthly parents to the age of 12. Then, it became time for me to be about by heavenly Father's business. I began at a young age. I didn't have a lot of time to spend down here because I had to go back to heaven and wait for the time to come back again. In the mean time I went about doing as I was taught by my earthly parents and by the Holy Spirit. My earthly father, Joseph, was a builder, a carpenter by trade. My heavenly Father is the Master Builder by trade, so I'm a carpenter's son who is also a master builder by trade. It's in my genes; it's in my blood.

"Before starting on my masterpiece, I was baptized in the Jordan River, and, being full of the Holy Spirit, was led by the Spirit into the wilderness. After fasting 40 days and 40 nights, I was put through a temptation routine by the devil. After passing the test, I began my ministry by praying always. I went about preaching, teaching, healing, and raising the dead back to life. I loved my work so well that I chose 12 men of mine own creation to work with me. Knowing that I would not be with them long, I revealed to them many things about myself and my work. I told them that I was going away to build a place so that they could be with me always. But, before I go I am going to build me a church. Because it will be my own church, I'm going to build it on myself, and 'the gates of hell shall not prevail against it' (Matt. 16:18). I will be the foundation, 'For other foundation can no man lay that that which is laid, which is Jesus Christ' (I Corinthian 3:10). Not only am I the foundation, but I am also the Head (Ephesians 1:22; Colossians 1:18)), the Door (John 10:9), and the Chief Corner Stone (Isaiah 28:16; I Peter 2:6), and even, 'You also as living stones are built up a spiritual house'" (I Pet. 2:5).

I want you to know that the work you do will speak for you, so be careful how you build on the foundation and watch the materials you use. When I was younger, I used to desire a brick house because I thought that if I had a brick house, it would never need anything else done to it. Then I heard about tuck pointing; we call it plain old chinking up the cracks. It seems as if even bricks wear away and will not stand up to the test. Your work will be tested by fire to show its real quality. If what was built on the foundation survives the fire, you, the builder now, will receive a reward. But if your work, brother or sister builder, is burned up, then you will lose out even though you yourself will be saved (I Cor.3:12-15). So, Saints, let us as laborers together with Christ build on love, for love is eternal; love will abide forever and will not burn up. Along with love use some joy, some peace, some gentleness, some goodness, some faith, and some good works as good building materials that will not burn. Also add some faith and hope which will abide and endure; "Now abides faith, hope, charity, these three, but the greatest of these is charity" (I Cor. 13:13). Love will help us to more effectively use the gifts that the Holy Spirit has set in the Church, which is the building. He did this to prepare all of God's people for the work of Christian service in order to build up the body of Christ. Under His control all of the different parts of the body fit together, and the whole body is held together by every joint with which it is provided. So, when each separate part works as it should, the whole body grows and builds itself up through love; even faith works by love (Galatians 5:6).

I myself am not a skilled laborer, so I'm working here on earth for the Master under the headship of the Holy Spirit, but my true citizenship is in heaven, in the city whose builder and maker is God. So, when "this earthly house of this tabernacle were dissolved, [I[have a building of God, an house not made with hands, eternal in the heavens" (II Cor. 5:1). I depend on God, The Master Builder, the one who built a stairway to the stars, the one who built a highway to heaven. "And now, [sisters and brothers], I commend you to God, and to the word of his grace, which is able to build you up, and to give you an inheritance among all them who are sanctified" (Acts 20:32). Amen.

THE FORMULA FOR TRIUMPHANT FAITH:EAT CROW + CARRY CROSS = WEAR CROWN

Psalm 27:1

Psalm 27:1 - *The Lord is my light and my salvation; whom shall I fear? The Lord is the strength of my life; of whom shall I be afraid?*

The scripture is taken from the Book of Psalms which is a connecting link between the Old and the New Testaments. No other book in the Bible more truly magnifies the word of God; it was written more for the saint than for the sinner.

However, let us begin with Ecclesiastes 3:1 which tells us, "To everything there is a season, and a time to every purpose under the heaven." Chapter 3:11 declares, "He has made everything beautiful in its time; also he has set the word in their heart, so that no man can find out the work that God makes from the beginning to the end." I Corinthians 14:40 says, "Let all things be done decently and in order." Yes, God is a timely God, and He does things decently and in order. Although the command for decency and order was to man, God Himself works on the same principle, system, method, formula, way or whatever word you choose. Even in the creation, notice the order and sequence. Darkness was everywhere; it stands to reason that you work better in the light than in the dark, ("I must work the work of him that sent me while it is day; the night comes, when no man can work," John 9:4). So God said, "Let there be light" (Genesis 1:3). In all of God's creation and works there is order, nothing chaotic about it. When man fell from his holy state, God, in His infinite wisdom, secured man's salvation by using the formula-"If you will obey [. . .]." Down through the dispensations God has always made a way for man's salvation. Now, He uses the formula, "I will [. . .]."

Even man, in his finite wisdom, works decently and in order by a formula. In chemistry H_2O is the formula for water. In algebra $(a + b)^2 = a^2 + 2ab + b^2$. In math you get percentages by multiplication. To get ¼, ½ , ¾, or any fraction, you divide. In the kitchen it's a recipe; in the pharmacy it's a prescription. Notice, if you please, that in all dispensations the requisite for salvation has always been faith. Hebrews 11:6 tells us, "But without faith it is impossible to please him; for he that comes to God must believe that he is, and that he is a rewarder of them that diligently seek him."

Here, in this 27th Psalm, in its entirety, we find the man, David, full of unwavering trust and gives a testimony that cannot be broken about the God of his salvation. Yes, I get joy and an increase in my faith when reading about how David from a youth up knew about the Lord. He gave his resume' to King Saul in I Samuel 17:31-37 about his ordeal when he was keeping his father's sheep: a lion and a bear took a lamb, and God delivered him out of the paw of the lion and the bear while he was rescuing the lamb. He had Saul to know that God would deliver him out of the hands of the uncircumcised Philistine, Goliath. This same David went on to be a warrior of unheard of bravery, a military genius, brilliant statesman, poet, musician, and, with all of his heart, a lover of God. This man of so great faith declares in Psalm 27:1, "The Lord is my light and my salvation (declaration) whom shall I fear (question)? The Lord is the strength of my life; (question) of whom shall I be afraid?" My subject is "The Formula For Triumphant Faith: Eat Crow + Carry Cross = Wear Crown."

My friends, in the general sense of the word, none of us likes to eat crow, humble pie, or take the low road. It is sometimes stated that the crow makes a lot of noise, but when the action comes, he's gone. Sometimes we have to eat our own words. We make statements like, "I'm not going to ..., I will not . . ., Ain't no way . . . ," but when we are confronted with the issue, we right away eat crow, " No, I didn't say that, not me." We eat our own words.

A good example of this is found in Luke 22:31-34 when the Lord said, "Simon, Simon, behold, Satan hath desired to have you, that he may sift you as wheat; But I prayed for you, that your faith fail not. And when you are converted, strengthen your brothers. And he (Peter) said unto him, Lord I am ready to go with you both into prison, and to death. And he (Jesus) said, I tell you, Peter, the cock shall not crow this day, before that you shall thrice deny that you know me." Further down in verses 54-62 we find that Peter had to eat crow or eat his own words. Peter didn't have the Faith yet, "And Peter went out and wept bitterly" (vs. 62) after denying Christ. He did repent for this great sin.

This is really what we have to do. When we can see ourselves, when we can see our shortcomings, then we can pray and ask the Lord to increase our faith (Lk. 17:5). Yes, our faith is going to be tested. The purpose of the testing is found in James 1:3-4, "Knowing this, that the trying of your faith works patience. But let patience have her perfect work, that you may be perfect and entire, wanting nothing." My friends we must toil on; we can't stop now. We cannot allow Satan to throw our shortcomings into our face and keep us from growing. We must go on unto perfection, growing in grace and in the knowledge of our Lord and Savior Jesus Christ. When we learn better, we can do better. So, we might have to eat a little crow until we learn to humble ourselves before God.

We must also learn to do as Jesus said in Mark 8:34, "Whosoever will come after me, let him deny himself, and take up his cross, and follow me." Cross bearing is something all of God's children will have to do; that's why it's part of the formula -- Eat Crow + Carry Cross = Wear Crown. In order for the formula to work, you have to do it; apply it to your lives. If you have the formula and won't live by it, you will not get the end results which is to wear a crown. So, my children, let us not be ashamed to carry the cross because "Jesus, the author and finisher of our faith, who for the joy that was set before him endured the cross, despising the shame, and is set down at the right hand of the throne of God" (Hebrews 12:2). Cross carrying is necessary just like preaching the gospel. Paul says in I Corinthians 9:16, "For though I preach the gospel, I have nothing to glory of; for necessity is laid upon me; woe is unto me, if I preach not the gospel!" What gospel? the gospel of the reconciling work of Christ, "And having made peace through the blood of his cross, by him to reconcile all things unto himself" (Colossians 1:20).

Yes, people, remember that there is a season and a time for all things. The season is now and it is time for us to stop following Jesus by remote control. It is time for us to make some moves for the Lord. It's time for us to stand on God's word; it's time for us to lay down on God's word; it's time for us to stretch out on God's word so that one day we will get up on God's word in that great getting up morning. Dare to be a Daniel or dare to say, like Daniel, The God I serve is able to deliver me" from whatever your lion's den is whether it is a drug habit, lust habit, lying habit or whatever. Dare to stand; dare to have a purpose; dare to make it known. Let us stand firm in the faith because it took faith to save you, and it takes faith to keep you. It takes faith in your daily living and faith in your dying. "Now abides these three, faith, hope and love" (I Cor. 13:13). Faith abideth forever, so let us stop brooding about the Dow Jones Averages falling, gas prices rising, and wars going on because the God we serve is able to sustain us. As David said in Psalm 37:25, "I have been young, and now am old; yet I have not seen the righteous forsaken, nor his seed begging bread."

Get on up and be about the business of cross bearing; put off, put on, study, walk, and last but not least, run. We have been walking long enough; it's running time. We are in the home stretch and have got to give it all we got. We don't want our running to be in vain. We don't want to stand before God, and He tells us, "You did run well; who did hinder you that you should not obey the truth?" (Galatians 5:7). My brothers and my sisters, in the words of a song, "I used to laugh at the saints of God every time I'd see them shout; I used to laugh when they kneeled down to pray, but look at me, I'm one of them today; that's because I'm sanctified now." I have truly "come this far by faith, leaning on the Lord. Trusting in His Holy word, He's never failed me yet." I know that God is faithful, and He keeps all of His promises.

It's up to me to keep and use the formula, Eat Crow + Carry Cross = Wear Crown. This formula is good throughout a life time on into eternity. It is not completed until we reach the other side. So, I'm running because I know as in I Corinthians 9:24, "Know you not that they who run in a race run all, but one receives the prize?" So, I, too, run that I may obtain an incorruptible crown. Now, a crown is something that everybody would like to have naturally or spiritually. Crown means to make a king or queen, to honor or reward, to be on top of, cover the highest part of, to make perfect or complete, or add the finishing touches to. In Isaiah 28:1 we find that there is a crown of pride. In proverbs 12:4 a virtuous woman is a crown. Proverbs 17:6 tells us that "Children's children are the crown of old men." In Matthew 27:28 a crown of thorns was put on Jesus' head. All of these crowns are corruptible; they, too, shall pass.

Saints, when I stand before my God, I want to hear him say well done. Then I want to get my crown. Saints, according to Scripture there are five (5) crowns obtainable:

1. A crown of life, James 1:12,
2. A crown of righteousness, II Timothy 4:18,
3. A crown of glory, I Peter 5:14,
4. A crown of rejoicing, I Thessalonians 2:19, and
5. An incorruptible crown, I Corinthians 9:25.

Out of all these crowns, I shall wear a crown. So, saints, remember the formula, and use it to obtain the crown. You won't get it on this side, but on the other side of the river. Now, listen to these words of a song: "Soon one morning, early one morning, I'm going to lay down my cross and get my crown." Amen.

WORKING TOGETHER IN UNITY: THE THIRD INGREDIENT

Psalm 133:1

Psalm 133:1 - *Behold, how good and how pleasant it is for brothers to dwell together in unity!*

We find that the psalms are a prayer book and hymnal of God's people. The Hebrew title for the psalter is Book of Praise. Worship, praise, confession, and outpouring of prayer characterize the Jewish people, and Psalms is also the prayer and praise manual of the Christian church. There is more than one theme of the psalms, but the basic theme is "The Spiritual conflicts and triumphs of saints under the old economy." The psalms also reflect the conflicts of God's people in every age. In classification there are five books. Our theme scripture comes from book five which contains Psalms 107-150. The 133rd Psalm, from which our scripture is taken, is called an ascent psalm. The ascent psalms were recited or sung as the pilgrims went up to Jerusalem to celebrate the feasts. The author of this psalm is David, who said or sung, "Behold, how good and pleasant it is for brothers to dwell together in unity" (Ps. 133:1).

In our theme scripture the psalmist is giving a brief praise on unity and brotherly love. He is telling of the pleasantness of dwelling together as having one heart, one soul, one interest. If I were to use a subject, it would be "The Third Ingredient." The number three in Scripture is the number of union, approval, approbation (proof) coordination, completeness, and perfection. The word unity means oneness. Oneness means union or harmony.

Genesis 1:1 says, "In the beginning God created the heaven and the earth." Verse 26 goes on to say, "And God said, Let us make man in our image, after our likeness; and let them have dominion over the earth, air, and sea." We find that man was made in the "image and likeness" of God. This image is found chiefly in the fact that man is a personal, rational, and moral being. God is infinite, and man is finite with limitations; nevertheless, man possesses the elements of personality similar to those of the divine person: thinking (Gen. 2:19-29; 3:8), feeling (Gen. 3:6), and willing (vs. 6-7). According to I Thessalonians 5:23 man is triune, made up of body, soul, and spirit, but because God is a Spirit (John 4:24), this tripartite nature of man is not to be confused with the original "image and likeness" of God. Man's spirituality relates to the elements of personality.

The Bible is a unity, and the purpose of God is one. Man, created in God's image, was placed in sovereignty over the earth, crowned with glory and honor yet subject to God, his creator (Gen.2:15-17). The divine intention was, and is, that man should have fellowship with God in obedience. Sin came; the essence of which is rebellion against the will of God. Man became separated from God (3:8-10) and lost sovereignty over the earth (vs. 17-19). The goal of God is to restore sinning man to His (God's) likeness, to restore fellowship with God, and to restore man's dominion over the earth. But, now, we see not yet all things put under him (mankind), but we see Jesus -- crowned with glory and honor in anticipation of many sons sharing God's fellowship and dominion (Hebrews 2:8-10; Romans 8:17-19). This fellowship and dominion is available to us by God's grace through faith. "It is because of the Lord's mercies that we are not consumed, because his compassions fail not" (Lamentations 3:22). This I am grateful for because if it had not been for God's mercy and compassion, He would not have given His only begotten Son to die for a world of sinners like me. Not only that, Jesus also said in John 8:28-29, "I do nothing of myself; but as my Father has taught me, I speak these things. And he that sent me is with me: the Father has not left me alone; for I do always those things that please him."

My friends, we do not know how this oneness is obtained, but we do believe God's holy word, for it says in John 10:30, "I and my Father are one." We know that in Scripture the number "3" is union, and union is oneness. In The Trinity we have the Father, the Son, and the Holy Ghost.

"There are three that bear record in heaven, the Father, the word, and the Holy Ghost: and these three are one. And there are three that bear witness in earth, the Spirit, and the water, and the blood; and these three agree in one" (I John 5:7-8). There are three definitions of God: God is Love, God is Light, and God is Spirit. There are three offices of Christ: prophet, priest, king. There is a three-fold truth of salvation: past--justification; present--transformation; future--consummation. There are three gifts of grace: faith, hope, love. Faith speaks of our own dependence; hope speaks of our own lack; love speaks to us of God. Faith is an imitation of God; hope is the aspiration to God; love is the manifestation of God. Faith and hope acquire blessings, but love bestows blessings. Before hope and faith, Love said, "I am." Love was before the world; love is eternal. Love is the nature and whole of God. I John 3:1a tells me, "Behold what manner of love the Father hath bestowed upon us."

Yes, I thank God that unity with God is available to all that will receive. I will give three illustrations of this unity. One is the vine and branches shown in John 15:1,5, "I am the true vine and my Father is the vinedresser [. . .]. I am the vine, you are the branches. Abide in me, for without me you are nothing." Another is the foundation and building as in I Corinthians 3:10-11; Ephesians 2:20-21, "I have laid the foundation, and another builds upon it. For other foundation can no man lay than that which is laid, which is Jesus Christ. There is also the unity of the husband and wife as in Ephesians 5: 25-32, "Husbands love your wives, even as Christ also loved the church, and gave himself for it."

Thank God for Jesus who has made it possible that all who partake in His death will partake of His resurrection. He is away now making preparation to come back for His bride, the Church, who is espoused to Him as a pure virgin. Jesus' bride, the church, will not be like Israel, God's wife, who solemnly swore that they would love the Lord their God with all their heart. Even after God told them that He was a jealous God, and for them, Israel, God's wife, to have no other gods before Him, they forsook Him, and went a whoring after other gods. This caused a separation. One day they will be restored, but we who are born again are waiting until the Bridegroom, Christ, comes to rapture out the church. While we are waiting, Jesus will not have any hanky-panky like Israel, God's wife. So he, Jesus Himself is building His church upon Himself. He told Peter, "Upon this rock I will build my church" (Matthew 16:18).

The church, which is Jesus, is built upon truth; this truth is that Jesus Christ is the Son of the living God. As such, Christ is sanctifying and cleansing the church "with the washing of water by the word, That He (Jesus) can present it to himself, a glorious church, not having spot, or wrinkle, or any such thing; but that it should be holy and without blemish" (Ephesians 5:26-27).

My friends, Christ is the head of the church, and all born again persons from Pentecost to the first resurrection (I Cor. 15:52) are united together and united to Christ by the baptism with the Holy Spirit (12:12-13) and make up the body of Christ. As such, the church is a holy temple for the habitation of God through the Spirit (Eph. 2:21-22), is one flesh with Christ (5:30-31), is espoused to Him as a pure virgin to one husband (II Cor. 11:2-4); and will be translated to heaven at the return of the Lord to the air (I Thessalonians 4:13-17).

As the Bride of Christ, "the marriage of the Lamb" is the consummation of the marriage of Christ and the church as his bride. This is in three stages:

1. the betrothal which is legally binding when the individual members of the body of Christ are saved;

2. the coming of the bridegroom for His bride at the rapture of the church; and

3. the marriage supper of the Lamb occurring in connection with the second coming of Christ to establish His millennial kingdom. At this time God's wife, Israel will be restored.

My friends, I am looking forward to that day. One thing for sure, I know I can't get jilted; I know a marriage will take place. I know it won't be "until death do us part." I know I will "live happily ever after." I know I got a mansion. I know I will never get sick; I know I will never grow old. I know all of these things because I got His Word, and I am doing just as He has instructed me. I considered the ant, and I'm making preparation; the coney, and I'm building on the rock; the locust, and I'm working together in unity with the brethen; the spider, and I'm determined (Proverbs 3:25-28). I also have The Third Ingredient, the Holy Ghost, which enables us to dwell together in unity. I'm working in unity with the spiritual leaders, and using the spiritual weapons the way God instructed. I say to you in the words of a song, "Bless be the tie that binds our hearts in Christian love; the fellowship of kindred minds is like to that above." Amen.

WE LIVE WITH THE PROBLEMS; WE WORK ON THE ANSWERS

John 6:67-69

John 6:67-69 - *Then said Jesus unto the twelve, will you also go away? Then Simon Peter answered him, Lord, to whom shall we go?" You have the words of eternal life, and we believe and are sure that you are that Christ, the Son of the living God.*

My friends, we have had problems in the world since Genesis the third chapter which records the temptation and fall of man. Because of good and evil, right and wrong, ups and downs, faithfulness and unfaithfulness, man found out early that he needed someone besides himself to lean on. In Genesis 4:26 man began "to call upon the name of the Lord." The old patriarchs who had faith relied on and prayed to God when they had problems, and God gave them the answers.

II Kings 6:8-17 tells the story of Elisha and his servant. Elisha had revealed the plans of the King of Syria to Israel. The Syrian king was troubled about it, so he called his servants wanting to know which of them was for the King of Israel; he thought they were revealing his plans. The servants assured the king it was none of them; it was Elisha, the man of God. The King of Syria told his servants to go and find out where Elisha was so he could capture him. "And it was told him, saying, Behold he is in Dothan. Therefore sent he there horses and chariots, and a great host; and they came by night, and compassed the city. And when the servant of the man of God was risen early and gone forth, behold, a host compassed the city, both with horses and chariots, and his servant said unto him (Elisha), alas, my master! What shall we do? And he answered, fear not; for they who are with us are more than they who are with them. And Elisha prayed, and said, Lord, I pray, open his eyes, that he may see. And the Lord opened the eyes of the young man, and he saw; and, behold, the mountain was full of horses and chariots of fire around Elisha" (vs. 13-17).

Yes, Elisha had problems; he worked on the answer. Where can we go? We have no other to whom we can turn. Even David, in Psalm 139:7-10, realized God's all-seeing eye and inescapable presence, for he said, "Where shall I go from your Spirit: or where shall I flee from your presence? If I ascend up into heaven, you are there; if I make my bed in hell, behold, you are there. If I take the wings of the morning, and dwell in the uttermost parts of the sea, even there shall your hand lead me, and your right hand shall hold me."

Yes, my friends, not only did the old patriarch saints pray and rely on God through faith but also New Testament, Latter Day, 20th century, and now 21st century saints as well. We all have to live with the problems, which is no surprise, for in John 16:33, Jesus said, "In the world you shall have tribulation, do not despair, but be of good cheer: I have overcome the world." So, even with the problems, we work on the answers. We who are the saved in the world are privileged to do this because we are in the army of the Lord, the Boss Man of the universe. We are affiliated with the Big Three, not the automobile makers but the Father, Son, and the Holy Ghost. We don't have the Good Housekeeping Seal of Approval; we have the seal of the Holy Spirit, and it's deep down in our heart. We can hold up holy hands; our feet can walk in a straight path; we don't have itching ears; our tongues can be tamed; and our aim is not the same because we have the Christ-like mind. I Corinthians 1:18 tells us, "For the preaching of the cross is to them that perish foolishness: but unto us who are saved it is the power of God." Yes, God's Word tells us; we don't have to hear it through the grapevine.

My friends, as we leave the 20th Century and enter the 21st century, we still live with problems. We are told that there is lead in the water, pollution in the air, and chemicals in the earth which penetrate our food. If that isn't enough, II Timothy 3:1-5 tells us, "This know, also, that in the last days perilous times shall come. For men shall be lovers of their own selves, covetous, boasters, proud, blasphemers, disobedient to parents, unthankful, unholy; without natural affection, trucebreakers, false accusers, incontinent, fierce, despisers of those that are good, traitors, heady, high-minded, lovers of pleasure more than lovers of God, having a form of godliness, but denying the power of it; from such turn away." With all of these problems in the world, God assures us in verses 11-14 that what persecutions we endure He can deliver us from all of them. "Yea all that will live godly in Christ Jesus shall suffer persecution (vs. 12). [. . .] But continue in the things that you have learned and have been assured of, knowing of whom you have learned them" (vs. 14).

People, we have problems, and we should be working on the answers. Before Jesus ascended up into the heavens, in Matthew 28:19-20 He gave the Great Commission: "Go, therefore, and teach all nations, baptizing them in the name of the Father, and of the Son, and of the Holy Ghost: Teaching them to observe all things whatsoever I have commanded you; and, lo, I am with you always, even unto the end of the world." Even with such a Great Commission for a world wide out-reach of the Gospel, Paul questioned, in Romans 10:14-16, how it was to be done, "How, then, shall they call on Him in whom they have not believed? And how shall they hear without a preacher: And how shall they preach, except they be sent: As it is written, How beautiful are the feet of them that preach the gospel of peace, and bring glad tidings of good things! But they have not all obeyed the gospel. For Isaiah said, "Lord, who has believed our report?"

Yes, yes, my friends, in these times everything is on the loose -- the pass word is loose; morals are loose; sex is loose; alcohol is loose; and suicide is loose. We have passed the Age of Aquarius and into the Age of Taurus; everything was bad and super bad, but even in this space age man still does not know that Jesus is the way, the truth, and the life. Man does not know that Jesus can give us the ability to stop wishing and start doing. It takes vision to dream big and a thirst for excellence and willingness to risk failure in order to succeed. Joy in doing is what makes all efforts worthwhile. Courage to get up off the floor and try again calls each of us to be, not just the best, but the best that we can be. More than that, millions have not heard that Jesus said, "I am the living bread that came down from heaven; if any man eat of this bread, he shall live forever" (John 6:51). If any man thirsts, let him come unto me, and drink (7:37). I am the door, by me if any man enters in, he shall be saved (10:9). If any man walks in the day, he stumbles not (11:9). If any man serves me, let him follow me" (12:26).

My brothers and my sisters, I heard the Good News when I was a child. At the age of twelve, Jesus spoke peace into my soul, gave me the same testimony as Simon Peter, "I believe and are sure that you are that Christ the Son of the living God," and sent me forth into His vineyard to work. My friends, the first thing all of us want to know when we are hired on a job is about the pay, the benefits, and is the job union or nonunion. On this job, as a spiritual laborer in God's vineyard, the pay is "whatever is right." The benefits are so numerous that David said, "Blessed be the Lord, who daily loads us with benefits" (Psalm 68:19), and, "What shall I render unto the Lord, for all his benefits toward me" (116:12).

Are we union or nonunion? I say to you tonight that all who fall in the category of workers in God's vineyard are full fledged union members, the head being Jesus Christ. Not only are we members of the union but also we are service members of the International Union which is headed by God the Father, God the Son, and God the Holy Ghost. Our Local number is 1-1-1. The International number is 1-6-1-1-1. One is God's number; six is man's number; and 1-1-1 is Father, Son, and Holy Ghost number. You can call anytime or anywhere; you can just ring them up in your heart. If you want to write, the address is City of God, 1-1-1 Straight Street, New Jerusalem. You can also write it in your heart.

We have our Constitution and By-Laws as revised and amended in the year of our Lord 1(one) A.D:

- Preamble: Every true laborer in God's vineyard can best be protected and advanced by their united action in one International Union.

- Article I: Name - One Lord, One Faith, One Baptism.

- Article II: Objects and purposes of this International Union shall be to benefit its members and improve their conditions by every means, including telling men, women, boys and girls that the wages of sin is death; the gift of God is eternal life.

- Article III: Jurisdiction and Membership - "Go into all the world, teach all nations, baptizing them in the name of the [International Union] Father, Son, and Holy Ghost."

- Article IV: Convention - The convention of this International Union shall meet every day, every month, and every year at such time and place as the International Executive Board may determine. The board consists of the one and same, as before stated, and may be referred to as the Trinity.

- Article V: Election of Officers - All nominations for International officers were made before there was a which, when, or where.

- Article VI: Officers - The officers of this International Union shall consist of the Father, Son, and the Holy Ghost.

- Article VII: Filling Vacancies - In the event of a vacancy in the office of the International Union by reason of death, it shall be the duty of the office to remain open until such time as the mission has been accomplished, the mission being to lay aside His glory, take on humanity, come down to earth, teach, preach, heal, raise the dead, die on a rugged cross to redeem man, lie in state in a borrowed tomb, and rise on the third day morning. When the mission is completed, He shall board a cloud and go back to glory to fill the vacancy.

Membership in the International Union requires fees. The cost of membership is to take up the cross and follow Christ. The union fees are for a born again Christian. Membership is more than lifetime but for all time and cannot be cancelled by evil men or tempting devils. However, just in case a member decides to walkout or to go on a wild cat strike, our intercessor and advocate, Jesus Christ is always there with outstretched arms pleading our case, telling the Father, "My blood is sufficient; I paid it all." You never have to send for any outside help, like Satan. Jesus Himself is our mediator, and every case is settled in the Internal Affairs Division of the International Union. To stay in good standing, just fear the Lord and keep His commandments.

My friends, since we live with the problems and work on the answers, it behooves us to get all wrapped up, tied up, and tangled up in the International Union. One thing I do know is "that if our earthly house of this tabernacle were dissolved, we have a building of God, an house not made with hands, eternal in the heavens" (II Corinthians 5:1). This is the place that John said, "And I saw the holy city, New Jerusalem, prepared as a bride adorned for her husband" (Revelation 21:2). The city was four square with 12 gates, the wall "was of Jasper: the city was pure gold, like glass (vs. 18), and the glory of God lit up the city, and the Lamb is the light thereof. And the nations of them who are saved shall walk in the light of it (vs. 23-24), and nothing shall enter in to defile it" (vs. 27).

My friends, some people say that when they get in the city, they want to sit down with Abraham, Isaac, and Jacob; that's alright, but let me tell you what I would like to do. After I see the three who are one, I want to see my mother, and tell her, "Hello, Mother, I made it over!" I want to go sweeping through the city, see my father and all of my friends and loved ones. Then, maybe, I'll meet all of the other saints, and we'll sit down by the banks of the river. What a time! What a time! What a time!

Yes, while you live with the problems, and work on the answers, Rudyard Kipling gives some good advice for you in his poem,

"If"

If you can keep your head when all about you
Are losing theirs and blaming it on you,
If you can trust yourself when all men doubt you,
But make allowance for their doubting, too;
If you can wait and not be tired by waiting,
Or being lied about, don't deal in lies,
Or being hated, don't give way to hating
And yet don't look too good, nor talk too wise:

If you can dream-and not make dreams your master;
If you can think--and not make thoughts your aim,
If you can meet with Triumph and Disaster
And treat those two impostors just the same;
If you can bear to hear the truth you've spoken
Twisted by knaves to make a trap for fools,
Or watch the things you gave your life to, broken,
And stoop and build them up with worn-out tools;

If you can make one heap of all your winnings
And risk it on one turn of pitch and toss,
And lose, and start again at your beginnings
And never breathe a word about your loss,
If you can force your heart and nerve and sinew
To serve your turn long after they are gone
And so hold on when there is nothing in you
Except the will which says to them, "Hold on!"

If you can talk with crowds and keep your virtue,
Or walk with Kings -- nor lose the common touch,
If neither foes nor loving friends can hurt you,
If all men count with you, but none too much;
If you can fill the unforgiving minute with sixty seconds' worth of distance run,
Yours is the Earth and everything that's in it,
And -- which is more -- you'll be a man, my son!

My brothers and sisters, while living here in this old sinful world, my heart can sing when I pause to remember that a heartache is but a stepping stone along the road that's always winding upward; this troubled world is not my final home. These things on earth will dim and lose their value, but, if you recall, they're borrowed for just a little while. When these things on earth cause our heart to tremble, remember that up there they will only bring a smile. Until then my heart will go on singing with joy; with joy I'll carry on until the day my eyes behold the city, until the day God call's me home.

"Now unto him who is able to keep you from falling, and to present you faultless before the presence of his glory, with exceeding joy, to the only wise God, our Savior, be glory and majesty, dominion and power, both now and forever" (Jude 24-25). Amen.

A NEW BEGINNING

Acts 3:7-8, 16

Acts 3:7-8, 16 *-And he took him by the right hand, and lifted him up; and immediately his feet and ankle bones received strength. And he, leaping up, stood and walked, and entered with them into the temple walking, and leaping, and praising God. [. . .] And His name, through faith in his name, has made this man strong, whom you see and know; yea, the faith which is by him has given him this perfect soundness in the presence of you all.*

The writer of these words was Luke, the beloved physician (Colossians 4:14). The book of Acts is a continuation of the story begun in the Gospel of Luke. These books, Acts and Luke, are addressed to the same person, Theophilus. They are linked together in Acts 1:1 by the phrase, "the former treatise", meaning the Gospel of Luke, which concerns what "Jesus began both to do and teach." The Book of the Acts records the continuation of the ministry by "the apostles whom Jesus had chosen." Both books speak of the coming of the Holy Spirit, of the disciples as witnesses, and of the ascension of the Lord Jesus into heaven. The Book of the Acts is of highest importance because it is the only inspired account of the beginning and early work of the church and a beginning of the future ministry to be accomplished by His followers after the coming of the Holy Ghost. Acts 1:8 records the last words spoken by Jesus just before His ascension into heaven, "But you shall receive power after the Holy Spirit is come upon you; and you shall be witnesses unto me both in Jerusalem, and in all Judea, and in Samaria, and unto the uttermost part of the earth."

As we look at our theme, "A New Beginning", we find that the word "beginning" is a noun. All English schools know that a noun is the name of a person, place, or thing. The word "beginning" means a start, the time when anything begins, the first part, or the first cause. As we look further at the theme, one might ask the question, "Why a new beginning?" We that are believers in Christ and His Holy word know that in the beginning God created the heaven and the earth. Everything that He made was good and very good, including the first man and woman. We know that after the fall of man, sin entered into the world, and every person born thereafter was a sinner. Genesis 6:5 tells us, "God saw that the wickedness of man was great in the earth, and that every imagination of the thoughts of his heart was only evil continually." Romans 3:10-11 explains, "There is none righteous, no not one. There is none that understand; there is none that seeks after God."

However, Isaiah 64:4 states, "For since the beginning of the world, men have not heard, nor perceived by the ear, neither has the eye seen, O God, besides you, what he has prepared for him who waited for him." Isaiah 48:18, "Oh, that you had harkened to my commandments! Then had your peace been like a river, and your righteousness like the waves of the sea." These verses give us the reason for "a new beginning"; there must be a change. Matthew 18:3 tells us, "Except you be converted and become as little children, you shall not enter the Kingdom of heaven." In order for man to change, John 3:16 says, " For God so loved the world, that He gave His only begotten son, that whosoever believeth in Him, should not perish, but have everlasting life." The requisite for man to be saved has always been faith in God, belief in God, and the shedding of blood. Without these there is no forgiveness of sin; therefore, they are of uttermost importance for "a new beginning".

In our scriptures for the theme, Peter and John are going to the temple at the hour of prayer. As they were about to go into the temple, they saw a certain man (no name) who was crippled from birth, whom they laid daily at the gate. The Bible gives no account of who "they" were, just that they laid him everyday at the gate called Beautiful. Why would they leave this lame man at the gate? According to *Unger's Bible Dictionary* gates were used as the entrance to enclosed grounds, buildings, cities, etc. These gates had various names such as fish gate, sheep gate, water gate, prison gate, King's gate, temple gate, etc. The purpose for the gates was for great assemblies of the people (Proverbs 1:27), as they passed into and out of the city or the other named gates. This led to the custom of using gates as places for public debates, reading the law and proclamations, holding court, gathering news, and gossip. Dignitaries were seen as they went in and out of the gates; priests and prophets delivered their sermons, admonitions and prophecies at the gates. In the figurative there are the gates of righteousness, the gates of death, and the gates of hell. We can see that gates were very important; in fact, according to Revelation 21:12 there are twelve (12) gates to the city of the New Jerusalem. We also have the strait gate to life.

So, it was at the gate called Beautiful that this crippled beggar was laid. In contrast Lazarus, a sick beggar, was laid at the rich man's gate. The man at the gate called Beautiful was crippled not by an accident but was born so; he was lame from his mother's womb. Pitiful cases like these show us what we are by nature spiritually; we are all without strength, lame from our birth, and unable to work or to walk in God's service. This man, crippled and unable to work for a living, begged. It is no disgrace to ask for what you need, especially if you are unable or cannot find work to supply yourself. We as Christians should not only give to the less fortunate but also pray for them. When this crippled beggar saw Peter and John about to go into the temple, he asked for alms.

The man asked for alms, but got a cure. Peter and John, instead of turning their eyes away from the beggar, fastened their eyes upon him and said, "Look on us." This gave the man reason to expect that he should receive something from them; therefore, he gave heed to them. This gives us to know that we must come to God with hearts fixed and expectations raised. The expectation of an alms was disappointed; Peter said, "Silver and gold have I none, but such as I have, give I thee. In the name of Jesus Christ of Nazareth, rise up and walk." My friends, I found out that money wouldn't change this man's condition, but Jesus did. Peter and John didn't have what the beggar wanted, but they had what he needed. Peter took him by the right hand and lifted him up. All of us may need a helping hand sometime; we don't have to do it by ourselves. There are other Christians to help you. When they reach out to you, don't turn away, but latch on and be lifted up. Notice, if you please, he took the man by the right hand which denotes the symbol of power and strength (Exodus 15:6; Psalm17:7). Holding by the right hand was expressive of support. The right hand of fellowship (Galatians 2:9) is given to all that accept Christ's grace to go out and do services for Him. Peter "lifted him up; and immediately his feet and ankle bones received strength." Yes, Jesus declared in John 12:32, "And I, if I be lifted up from the earth, will draw all men unto me." Love lifted the man. The call is to whosoever will because the gates of mercy stand open-- wide open. The beggar, "leaping, stood and walked, and entered with them into the temple, walking and leaping and praising God." This shouting was the effect that the cure had on this lame man. I tell you if I had been there, I would have shouted, too. I know the angels shouted. You can shout right now if you want to; it's alright. I imagine the man might have sung this verse of a song, "What a wonderful change in my life has been wrought, since Jesus came into my heart." Not only did the man shout, but he went into the temple with Peter and John; he wouldn't let go. I don't blame the man; that's where the saved, the healed or any miracle receiver should be, at church, a place where there is always an outstretched hand to lift you when you need it. God said in Hebrews 10:25, "[. . .] not forsaking the assembling of yourselves together." This healing should have been a great time for testimony service.

After this great miracle, the people were so amazed and full of wonder. When Peter saw it, he preached his second sermon. He had preached the first sermon on the Day of Pentecost as recorded in the 2nd chapter; this event was a few days later. In this sermon as recorded in this 3rd chapter, Peter had them to know in verses 13 and 16, "The God of Abraham, and of Isaac, and of Jacob, the God of our fathers, has glorified his Son Jesus whom you delivered up and denied in the presence of Pilate when he was determined to let him go. [. . .] And his name, through faith in his name, has made this man strong, whom you see and know; yea the faith which is by him has given this perfect soundness in the presence of you all." This man truly had a new beginning.

My brothers and sisters, as children of God, let us lay aside all things that are not like Christ; we cannot filibuster, sabotage, or use subtlety and please God. We must be fair, just, and honest in all our dealings. What you measure out will be measured back to you. Let us work hard doing what "thus said the Lord." We have the power and authority to do many things just as Peter and John did, but we don't have anything to brag about. When Jesus sent the 70 (seventy) out, He told them what to do and what not to do. When they came back, they were rejoicing saying, "Lord even the (demons) are subject unto us through your name." Jesus told them, "I beheld Satan as lightning fall from heaven, Behold I give unto you power to tread on serpents and scorpions and over all the power of the enemy;

and nothing shall by any means hurt you. Notwithstanding, in this rejoice not, that the spirits are subject unto you; but, rather rejoice because your names are written in heaven" (Luke 10:17-20).

Yes, yes, my friends, the time is now to serve the Lord. Hebrews 12:l tells us, "Wherefore, seeing we also are compassed about with so great a cloud of witnesses, let us lay aside every weight and the sin which does so easily beset us and let us run with patience the race that is set before us." Let us join hands and hearts together, knit in by a bond of strong love that Satan cannot penetrate. Let us not forget that Jesus, our Lord and Savior, prayed to the Father for us when He said, " Holy Father, keep through your own name those whom you have given me that they may be one as we are. [. . .] I pray not that you should take them out of the world, but that you should keep them from the evil. [. . .] Neither pray I for these alone, but for them also who shall believe on me through their word" (John 17:11, 15, 20).

This same Jesus who prayed for us has ascended into heaven and is seated on the right hand of the Father. This same Jesus has gone to prepare a place for all whom He prayed for to be with Him. This same Jesus, the world's greatest mathematician, took two (2) fish, and five (5) loaves of bread, gave thanks to the Father, multiplied, and divided it among over 5,000 people, and then added up what was left. This same Jesus whom Peter preached about after the lame man was healed is the same Jesus whom they hung high and stretched wide, who hung His head for me and died.

This same Jesus is the one whom I heard someone say that Death and the Grave had a talk about. After Jesus declared, "It is finished!" When he dropped his head between the locks of His shoulders and "gave up the Ghost", they tell me that Death went by the Grave and told the Grave, "I got Him; you keep Him."

Well Grave told Death, "I'll do all I can to hold Him. I thought I had Lazarus, but after four days, this same Jesus raised him up."

"Well," Death said, "I had a few mishaps myself. I tried hard to get Enoch, but he walked too fast. I tried hard to get Elijah, but he rode too fast, so let's keep our fingers crossed." Well, the first day Death went by the grave, he asked, "Grave, you got Him?"

Grave said, "Yes, I got Him."

Death asked, "Can you hold Him?

Grave said, "Yes, I can hold Him."

The second (2nd) day Death went by the grave and asked, "Grave, you got Him."

Grave said, "Yes, I got Him."

Death asked again, " Can you hold Him?"

Grave said," I told you I got Him, and if I got Him, I can hold Him!"

On the third (3rd) day Death decided to check one more time. Death went by the grave and asked, "Grave, you got Him?

Grave said, "No, I don't have Him; I couldn't hold Him. I really tried hard, but He got up and told me that 'all power is given unto me in heaven and earth,' (Matthew 28:18). Do you think He was bragging when he added, 'Can't no power on earth hold me down; Death can't keep me in the ground.' Then He gave me a message for both of us, 'Death is swallowed up in victory. O death, where is your sting? O grave where is your victory?'" (I Corinthians 15:54).

Yes, my friends, this same Jesus hung, bled, died, rose in my behalf, and one day is coming back for me. One of these old days, when it's all over, like the words of a song:

"This old soul of mine is going home to live with my God. . . . That morning, when I rise, I'll shake the dust from my feet, And God will wipe the tears from my eyes. What a day that's going to be, by and by."

That's when all of God's children will be together, and it's all because of a man called Jesus. Jesus, who was hung high, stretched wide, hung His head, for me He died and rose again, is coming back for all who trusted Him so they can have "A New Beginning."

A CHARGE TO KEEP I HAVE

II Timothy 4:1-2

II Timothy 4:1-2 - *I charge you therefore before God, and the Lord Jesus Christ, who shall judge the living and the dead at his appearing and his kingdom; preach the word; be diligent in season, out of season; reprove, rebuke, exhort with all longsuffering and doctrine.*

The writer of this epistle was Paul. This epistle along with I Timothy and Titus are called pastorals because they were written to pastors and discuss chiefly the duties of pastors. Pastorals were not written to churches but to individuals. The place of this writing was from the Mamertime Dungeon during Paul's final imprisonment in Rome under Nero. The occasion for the writing: Paul was begging Timothy to be faithful as many of his friends had deserted him and departed from his teachings.

We find that the name Timothy means "he who honors God." This name probably reflects the hope of his mother Eunice and grandmother Lois. The word "charge" means to lay or put load on or in; to impose a task or responsibility on; accuse; blame; to bring into position for attack; or to ask payment of a person. The synonym for the word "charge" is a command. So, we see that a charge is a great responsibility. Today, we are speaking about a spiritual charge. In the beginning of creation, as God finished His creations, He gave a charge. On the first day He charged day to furnish light and night to furnish darkness. Each day as He created and made, God gave a charge. On the sixth day God came together with the God Head and said, "Let us make man." After making man God gave man a charge to "Be fruitful and multiply and fill the earth, subdue it, have dominion over the fish of the sea, over the fowl of the air and over every living thing that moves upon the earth" (Genesis 1:28).

Down through the different generations God has given different ones of His servants "a charge to keep." In Exodus 6:13, "The Lord spoke unto Moses and Aaron and gave them a charge unto the children of Israel and unto Pharaoh, King of Egypt, to bring the children of Israel out of the land of Egypt." Not only does God give charges but He also gives official authority to others to give a charge. I Kings 2:1-3 states, "Now the days of David drew near that he should die; and he charged Solomon his son saying, I go the way of all the earth: be strong therefore, and show yourself a man; And keep the charge of the Lord your God, to walk in His ways, to keep his statutes, and his commandments and his judgments and his testimonies, as it is written in the law of Moses, that you may prosper in all that you do, and wherever you turn yourself."

We see Paul, in II Timothy, giving a charge to Timothy. He states the charge in these awesome words: "I charge you therefore before God, and the Lord Jesus Christ," Paul is letting him know that this is no plaything. As he gives the charge, Paul reminds Timothy of the judgment to come. Paul tells him to "Preach the word;" this is a minister's business. To urge Timothy in what he preached, Paul tells him to "be instant in season and out of season, reprove, rebuke, exhort: do this work with all fervency of spirit." In season is when some special opportunity presents itself; out of season is because you don't know when the Spirit of God will work. Tell the people of their faults, dealing plainly with them in order to bring them to repentance. He must direct and encourage those who began well, exhort with all longsuffering, and teach them the truth about Jesus. Not only that but he must watch in all things, in his work, against temptations of Satan, as well as watch over the souls of those committed to his charge. Yes, the pastor must count on afflictions and endure them; he must become used to hardships, must remember his office, and must discharge his duties. After these final instructions Paul goes on to tell Timothy the rewards for fighting a good fight and keeping the faith. Paul told how God had stood by him and strengthened him, "that by [Paul] the preaching [of the Gospel] might be fully known, and that all the Gentiles might hear; and [he] was delivered out of the mouth of the lion. And the Lord shall deliver [him] from every evil work and will preserve [him] unto his heavenly kingdom" (4:17-18).

My friends, this was Paul's charge to Timothy and to all pastors everywhere, but what about us who have not been called to pastor? Every believer in Christ Jesus is a member of His body with a definite ministry. Ephesians 4:7 tell us, "[. . .] but unto everyone of us is given grace according to the measure of the gift of Christ." Jesus said in Luke 19:10, "For the Son of man is come to seek and to save that which was lost," and in John 20:21, "As my Father has sent me, so send I you." This message is to all born again believers in Jesus Christ. Along with your special ministry we are all missionaries called to tell unsaved men, women, boys, and girls, "Repent and be baptized every one of you" (Acts 2:38).

Christ is depending on us, His followers, to carry out this mission, and He has given us the authority to do so by His words. In Matthew 5:13 we are told, "You are the salt of the earth, but if the salt has lost its savor, with what shall it be salted? It is therefore good for nothing, but to be cast out, and to be trodden under foot of men." We know that salt is small which is the way all Christians should be. Being small shows humbleness never getting too big for anything. Salt is white which denotes purity; we must be pure in our religion and just in all our dealings. Just as salt is good for seasoning and preserving food, we, as Christians, are responsible for seasoning the earth with the true and pure gospel, witnessing to sinners, and living Christ like to preserve some lost souls. Yes, we are the salt of the earth, and if we cease to season the earth, we are good for nothing; then who would melt the ice of sin; who would preserve the goodness of the Lord, and most importantly, who would show a wounded soul how to be healed by the love of God. We are still talking about "a charge to keep."

Yes, not only are we the salt of the earth but also we are the light of the world--we are not that light neither are we that salt--but we have similitude or similarities and are to bear witness of the same. In John 8:12 Jesus declared, "I am the light of the world; he that follows me shall not walk in darkness but shall have the light of life." Therefore, *we are* the light of the world because *we have* the light of life. In order to help us keep the charge, John 4:23-24 tells us, "But the hour comes, and now is when the true worshippers shall worship the Father in spirit and in truth; for the Father seeks such to worship him. God is a Spirit; and they that worship Him must worship Him in spirit and in truth." These verses tell us how to please God. Jesus died in order to purify the people from sin with His own blood; therefore, let us always offer praise to God for Jesus' sacrifice by confessing Him as Lord, not forgetting to do good, and helping one another. Yes, my friends, as we go from day to day in our Christian lives, we should present our bodies a living sacrifice, holy, acceptable unto God, and be not conformed to this world, but be transformed by the renewing of your mind for this is the will of God" (Romans 12:1-2). If God also sees fit to bless us material wise, I Timothy 6:17 tells us, "Charge them that are rich in this Age, that they be not high minded, nor trust in uncertain riches but in the living God, who gives us richly all things to enjoy."

Brothers and sisters, as children of God, in Matthew 7:7-8, God has given us the privilege to "Ask, and it shall be given you; seek, and you shall find; knock, and it shall be opened unto you. For every [Christian] that asks, receives; and he that seeks, finds; and to him that knocks it shall be opened." This privilege is based upon our relationship to God as the Father of all who truly believe on His Son. My friends, we all have a charge to keep if we expect to enter into the city whose builder and maker is God and if we expect to be as Daniel said in chapter 12:3, "And they that be wise shall shine like the brightness of the firmament; and they that turn many to righteousness, as the stars forever and ever." We must also "Put on the whole armor of God that we may be able to stand against the wiles of the devil." We can be assured that we will stand for God said in Romans 14:4, "Who are you that judges another man's servant? To his own master he stands or falls. Yea he shall be held up; for God is able to make him stand."

"We must fight the good fight of faith, lay hold on eternal life" (I Timothy 6:12), and don't let anybody turn you around. If we expect to ride the train to glory, we must be right; we must be saved; and we must be whole. We must keep on keeping on because as II Peter 1:14 says, "Knowing that shortly I must put off this body even as our Lord Jesus Christ has shown me." Yes, yes, my friends, the whole world has a charge to keep; even God Himself had a charge to keep. When man sinned, God gave Himself a charge to redeem man. In Genesis 3:15 God said, "And I will put enmity between you and the woman, and between your seed and her seed; he shall bruise your head, and you shall bruise his heel." Yes, sometimes in order to keep the charge, God would send an angel or some designated person, but for the redemption of man, God said in Ezekiel 22:30, "And I sought for a man among them, that should make up the hedge, and stand in the gap before me for the land, that I should not destroy it; but I found none." Therefore, a conference was held in glory; the three God Heads came together again about man. I can imagine in my mind the words that might have been said.

The Father said, "My first son, Adam, I made for the earth. I put him over all things on earth, but he has committed high treason, and Satan has taken over. Now, I will have to go down and redeem man."

I hear another voice saying, "Father, you don't have to go; I'll go. If I go, it will be like you going because you and I are one" (John 10:30).

So God came down through 42 generations (Matthew 1:17) and was born of a virgin named Mary in whom God had found favor (Luke 1:30). Yes friends, God kept His charge; there is no failure in God.

My sisters and brothers let us not be hard hearted and rebellious like Israel, for God gave them a charge to keep; they failed. As punishment God allowed the enemy to take them into captivity. While in captivity they cried, "By the rivers of Babylon, there we sat down, yea we remembered Zion. We hung our harps upon the willows in the midst thereof. For there they that carried us away captives required of us a song; and they that wasted us required of us mirth, saying, 'Sing us one of the songs of Zion.' How shall we sing the Lord's song in a foreign land?" (Psalm 137:1-4). This is the same results we have for not keeping the charge that God gives us; Satan will laugh at you and expect you to entertain Him.

As for me personally, God gave me a charge to keep. When I was 12 years old, He told me to believe and be baptized for the remission of sin. I was only a little girl, and it took me a long time to find out my true responsibility even though I had the charge. Down through the years, I was backsliding, stumbling, rising and falling, going up and down, but I still had that charge. Then one day God stabilized me and made me steadfast; then the charge became a reality. I began to pray and ask God what He wanted me to do. The message came through loud and clear, "Be my witness." Notice, if you please, when God gives you the charge, He adds to it. He doesn't take it back; He adds to it. God told us to add to our faith (II Peter 1:5). Later, after telling me to witness, God added teaching. Later He added healing, helps, prophetess, and discerning of spirits.

My brothers and my sisters, I am still trying, by the help of God and by the aid of the Holy Spirit, to keep the charge. When we keep the charge, we can say as Paul said in II Timothy 4:6-8, "For I am now ready to be offered and the time of my departure is at hand. I have fought a good fight, I have finished my course, I have kept the faith; Henceforth there is laid up for me a crown of righteousness, which the Lord, the righteous judge, shall give me at that day: and not to me only, but unto all them also that love his appearing." There are 5 (five) crowns that I know about mentioned in God's word:

- In I Thessalonians 2:19 there is a crown of rejoicing, so rejoice; it's alright;

- In James 1:12 the crown of life is given to those who endure temptation and love the Lord;

- In Revelation 2:10 this crown of life is for those who are faithful unto death;

- In I Peter 5:4 there is a crown of glory that will not fade away; and,

- Of course, there is crown of righteousness so get right and stay right; the Lord might come tonight.

My sisters and brothers, I may not get five crowns, but I *shall* wear a crown because I am persuaded that nothing shall separate me from the love of God. I'm going to "hold fast to what [I] have that no man take my crown" (Rev. 3:11). When I get my crowns, I will do as the four and twenty elders did in Revelation 4:10-11; I will "cast [my] crowns before the throne of God, and say, You are worthy, O Lord, to receive glory and honor and power; for you have created all things, and for your pleasure they are and were created." These crowns are the rewards talked about in Revelation 22:12 where God said, "And, behold I come quickly, and my reward is with me, to give every man according as his work shall be."

Yes, my friends, when we become saved, God gives us a charge to keep. If we fail to carry out the charge, it's our own fault, for there is no failure in God. We still have that charge, and God is holding us responsible for the charge that He gave us. If we persist in not keeping the charge, think on the words of a song about God's way that you can't go over; you can't go under; and you can't go around. You've got to come in at the door because as the song tells us:

He's the way, the truth and the life;

If you want to see Jesus, you have to live right.

You must be saved; come out of your sin.

Marvel not, you must be born again; thank you.

MAKING THE RIGHT CHOICE

Joshua 24:15

Joshua 24:15 - *And if it seem evil unto you to serve the Lord, choose you this day whom you will serve; whether the gods which your fathers served that were on the other side of the flood, or the gods of the Amorites, in whose land you dwell: but as for me and my house, we will serve the Lord.*

The author of the book of Joshua from which our theme is taken was, of course, Joshua. He wrote all except his death and burial. We find the name Joshua means Jehovah saves. We also find that Joshua's life, though recorded with fullness of detail, shows no stain. By the faithful serving of his youth, he was taught to command as a man; as a citizen he was patriotic in the highest degree; as a warrior he was fearless and blameless; and as a judge he was calm and impartial. He was quite equal to the task and ready for every emergency under which he was to act. He was valiant without being rash and active without haste. No care, no advantage, and no duty is neglected by him. He ever looked up for divine direction, obeyed divine direction with the simplicity of a child, and handled the great power given him with calmness, humility, and without swerving accomplishing a high, unselfish purpose. He earned by manly vigor a quiet, honored, old age and retained his faith and loyalty, exclaiming in almost his dying breath, "As for me and my house, we will serve the Lord!"

In our scripture text Joshua saw the value in calling the people to make a definite commitment, saying, "Choose you this day whom you will serve." Centuries later Elijah stood on Mt. Carmel challenging the people, "How long halt you between two opinions? If the Lord be God, follow him: but if Baal, then follow him" (I Kings 18:21). God is still calling for us to commit ourselves unto Him today. He tells us in James 4:7-8, 10, "Submit yourselves, therefore, to God, Resist the devil and he will flee from you. Draw near to God, and He will draw near to you. Cleanse your hands, you sinners; and Purify your hearts, you double minded. [. . .]. Humble yourselves in the sight of the Lord, and he shall lift you up."

Young people, God is also calling for commitments from you. I know that you may say within yourself, "I have a few more things I want to do," or, " I'm still young," but God tells us in His Holy Word in Ecclesiastes 12:1, "Remember now your creator in the days of your youth, while the evil days come not, nor the years draw near when you shall say, I have no pleasure in them." Yes, a choice must be made. Matthew 6:24 says, "No man can serve two masters: for either he will hate the one, and love the other: or else he will hold to the one, and despise the other. You cannot serve God and mammon." If you choose to live ungodly, that's your business, but if you choose to live godly, it's God's business. Our future has been determined by our own decisions, and the Lord has made it known what the judgment will be.

People, we who have chosen to serve the Lord must hold to God's unchanging hand because trouble will come; it's a must. II Timothy 3:12 says, "They that live godly must suffer persecution." Even with the persecution don't despair; have the determination that Paul had in II Corinthians 12:10, "Therefore, I take pleasure in infirmities, in reproaches, in necessities, in persecutions, in distress for Christ's sake; for when I am weak, then I am strong." We can also take heart from Caleb in the 14th chapter of Joshua. Caleb wanted Mt. Hebron as an inheritance in the land of promise. In verses 7-12 Caleb was forty years old when Moses sent him to spy out the land. At this time Moses had promised Caleb Mt. Hebron because this was the land that he had spied out. Moses was dead when they entered into the Promised Land, but Caleb didn't lose heart. He was 85 years old when he went to Joshua to ask for his inheritance. Caleb concludes by saying to Joshua, "I am as strong this day as I was in the day that Moses sent me: as my strength was then even so is my strength now, for war, both to go out, and to come in. Now, therefore, give me this mountain, of which the Lord spoke in that day; for you heard in that day how the Anakim were there, and that the cities were great and fenced; if so be the Lord will be with me, then I shall be able to drive them out, as the Lord said."

Yes, just as God gave the Israelites, his chosen people, an inheritance, we, too, as God's chosen people have an inheritance. Romans 8:14-17 tells us, "For as many as are led by the Spirit of God, they are the sons of God. For you have not received the spirit of bondage again to fear; but you have received the Spirit of adoption, whereby we cry, Abba, Father. The Spirit himself bears witness with our spirit, that we are the children of God; and if children, then heirs -- heirs of God, and joint heirs with Christ -- if so be we suffer with him, that we may be also glorified together." My friends, God has promised us an inheritance, but we, too, must fight for it, just as the Israelites did when they entered into the land of promise. It's yours just for the asking. Mark 11:22-23 says, "Have faith in God, for verily I say unto you, whosoever shall say unto this mountain, Be removed, and be cast into the sea; and shall not doubt in his heart, but shall believe that those things which he says shall come to pass, he shall have whatever he says." Then, we can do just as Caleb did; if we have faith, we can say, "Give me this mountain."

Luke 11:9-10 tells us, "Ask and it shall be given you" (This means pray the prayer of faith.); "seek and you shall find" (This means look for it with all of your heart.); "knock and it shall be opened unto you" (This means to drive, force, make, or drive out.). My brothers and sisters, all we have to do is ask, seek, knock, fight the good fight of faith, and don't give up. God will give it to you not only in this world but also in the world to come. Titus 2:11-14 tells us, "For the grace of God that brings salvation has appeared to all men, Teaching us that, denying ungodliness and worldly lusts, we should live soberly, righteously, and godly, in this present world; Looking for that blessed hope, and the glorious appearing of the great God and our Savior, Jesus Christ, Who gave himself for us, that he might redeem us from all iniquity, and purify unto himself a peculiar people, zealous of good works."

Sometimes you may have to run; that's alright, for I Corinthians 9:24 says, "Know you not that they who run in a race run all, but one receives the prize? So, run that you may obtain." Sometimes you may have to cry; that's alright, for David said in Psalms 120:1, "In my distress I cried unto the Lord, and he heard me." Sometimes you may have gone as far as you can go; that's alright, too; just stand and see the salvation of the Lord. Just don't give up; hang on in there for God has given you the battle. You don't have to wait 'til the battle is over; you can shout now; we've already won!

So, gird up you loins, put on all of the armor, and do everything that God told us to do in Ephesians 6:14-17. We are in God's army now, and

God doesn't want a coward soldier. He told us to endure hardness as a good soldier, and in the words of the late Dr. Martin Luther King, Jr., "There are some difficult days ahead." We know that this is true for II Timothy 3:1-4 says, "This know also, that in the last days perilous times shall come, For men shall be lovers of their own selves, covetous, boasters, proud, blasphemers, disobedient to parents, unthankful, unholy, without natural affection, trucebreakers, false accusers, incontinent, fierce, despisers of those that are good, traitors, heady, high minded, lovers of pleasure more than lovers of God, Having a form of godliness but denying the power of it; from such turn away." My friends, these days are here now, and we had better get right, for I can hear the approaching hoof beats of the four horsemen that were spoken of in Zechariah 6:1-7 and in Revelation 6:2-8:

- The white horse and its rider deceive from inside and outside the church. Don't get him confused with Christ who, in a later chapter in Revelation, will come on a white horse, too. You know Satan has the pretenders in church who act like the real people of God;
- The red horse rider makes war;
- The black horse rider brings hunger; and
- The pale horse rider brings pestilence and death.

I can hear in the distance the thundering hoof beats approaching bearing their riders of judgment. It behooves us to have made the right choice or else this judgment will fall on us.

My friends, we who have chosen to serve the Lord let us go forth in full assurance knowing in whom we have believed. Study God's word, and know what is required of us. God wants us to know about Him, for He said in Hosea 4:6, "My people are destroyed for lack of knowledge: because you have rejected knowledge, I will also reject you." It is also written, "Man shall not live by bread alone, but by every word that proceeded out of the mouth of God" (Matthew 4:4). Let us know who we are; know that we are children of God, made in His image and likeness. Let us progress toward maturity steadfast in the faith. Hebrews 6:1 tells us, "Therefore leaving the principles of the doctrine of Christ, let us go on unto perfection; not laying again the foundation of repentance from dead works, and of faith toward God." Some of us never get past the stage of "I know I've been born again." God knows it; you know it, so go on to higher heights and deeper depths in the Lord. "For God is not unrighteous to forget your work and labor of love, which you have shown toward his name, in that you ministered to the saints, and do minister" (vs. 10).

My friends, I want you to know that, just as Job says in Chapter 16:9, "My witness is in heaven, and my record is on high." People, my heart is fixed and my mind is made up to go all the way with the Lord. I intend to run on in Jesus' name. I'm trying to win the prize. I want you to know that I'm working in the vineyard, and that as a part of my labor, God has given me a voice to speak His divine message, for He told me that I am a prophet. He put healing in my hands; He's given me to minister to others in any way that I can. He's given me discerning of spirits which is being able to see in the spirit world--people, demons, angels, and Jesus. He's given me these things because I chose to serve him. Not only that but also He's got greater things for me. I Corinthians 2:9 says," But as it is written, eye has not seen, nor ear heard, neither have entered into the heart of man, the things which God has prepared for them that love him."

Romans 8:37 adds, "Nay in all things we are more than conquerors through him that loved us. For I (like Paul) am persuaded, that neither death, nor life, nor angels, nor principalities, nor powers, nor things present, nor things to come, nor height, nor depth, nor any other creature, shall be able to separate [me] from the Love of God, which is in Christ Jesus our Lord." People, my expectations are to be living and doing a good work when Christ comes. A lot of people say that we all are going to die, but not so for Christ said in I Corinthians 15:51-52, "Behold, I show you a mystery; We shall not all *sleep,* but we shall all be changed, In a moment, in the twinkling of an eye, at the last trump: for the trumpet shall sound, and the dead shall be raised incorruptible and we shall be changed."

Now, if I die before this happens, if you are still around, you can say that this was not her expectation. It has to be done like God wants it and not I. But, until then, my heart will go on singing. Until then, with joy, I'll carry on until the day my eyes behold that city, until the day God calls me home. Thank you.

WORKERS IN GOD'S VINEYARD

Matthew 20:4

Matthew 20:4 - *And said unto them; you also go into the vineyard, and whatsoever is right I will give you, and they went their way.*

The writer of this gospel is Matthew, also called Levi. He tells the good news that Jesus is the promised Savior, the one through whom God fulfilled the promises He made to His people in the Old Testament. This good news is not only for the Jewish, among whom Jesus was born and lived, but also for the whole world. Matthew begins with the birth of Jesus, describes his baptism and temptation, and then takes up His ministry of preaching, teaching, and healing in Galilee. After this the gospel records Jesus' journey from Galilee to Jerusalem and the events of Jesus' last week climaxing in His crucifixion and resurrection. This gospel presents Jesus as the great teacher who has authority to interpret the Law of God and who teaches in parables about the Kingdom of Heaven ending with his teachings about the end of the present age and the coming of the Kingdom of God.

We find in Chapter 19:27 Jesus telling this parable in answer to the question asked by His disciples concerning their forsaking all to follow Him. Jesus assured them that everyone who has forsaken all to follow Him will receive an hundred fold and shall inherit eternal life. After answering the question, He then tells the parable of the laborers in which were spoken these words: "And said unto them; you also go into the vineyard, and whatsoever is right I will give you, and they went their way." The parable of our lesson for tonight begins with the connective word "for" (vs. 1). The word "for" links with the last verse of Chapter 19 which says, "Many that are first shall be last; and the last shall be first" (vs. 30). At the end of our parable, we find similar words (20:16). So, the purpose of the parable was to move the disciples' viewpoint from future rewards to present responsibilities.

The parable begins saying, "For the Kingdom of heaven is like a man that is an householder, who went out early in the morning to hire laborers into his vineyard. And when he had agreed with the laborers for a penny a day, he sent them into his vineyard." We notice that Jesus begins by telling what the Kingdom of Heaven is like. We find in our research that most of the times the words "Kingdom of Heaven" are used when they have to do with a description of any type of ruling domain that God may assert on the earth at a given period. The Kingdom of God has to do with all created intelligences both in heaven and on earth. Some writers use both terms interchangeably. Jesus is telling this parable so that we will know what is expected of us in the Kingdom of Heaven which is on earth.

He tells about the householder who went out early in the morning to hire laborers into his vineyard. Well, what is a vineyard? A vineyard is a cultivated garden or field of which it takes a lot of preparation. First of all the vineyard is fenced or hedged around for protection by a permanent fence; no other crop requires this. Secondly, all of the larger stones are removed and heaped like a stone wall to let the vines trail on to protect the fruit from the dampness. The smaller stones are left to retain moisture in the ground. In the vineyard we also find a winepress and a watchtower. The winepress is used to extract the juices from the grapes. It is built with two parallel troughs with one being above the other having a perforated conduit or channel between them. The watchtower is used to guard the vintage from thieves.

We find that, as we look down through the dispensations of time, God has always been the householder, for He planted the vineyard, which is the world, made man, and gave him a charge to keep, dress, and replenish. During the course of time, a nation was born which was Israel. We find that the vine is a symbol of the nation of Israel. The vine was taken into Egypt, thus the vine, Israel was in the world; Egypt represents the world. Instead of doing as "thus said the Lord," Israel went out to play. Israel was not grateful for God's benefits. Hosea 11:1-2 says, "When Israel was a child, then I loved him, and called my son out of Egypt, As they called them, so they went from them: they sacrificed unto Baalim, and burned incense to graven images. I taught Ephraim (another term for Israel) also to go taking them by their arms: but they knew not that I healed them."

We find that the vine represents Israel in the vineyard which is the world. Israel is unfruitful so they were not brought to maturity; they were cut off as chastisement. They were considered as wild grapes. As time went on Jeremiah, sometimes called the weeping prophet, looked one day at the desperate state of his people and said, "The harvest is past, the summer is ended, and we are not saved. Is there no balm in Gilead; is there no physician there: Why then is not the health of the daughter of my people recovered?" (8:20-22). He continues, "Oh that my head were waters, and mine eyes a fountain of tears, that I might weep day and night for the slain of the daughter of my people!" (9:1).

My brothers and sisters, in spite of all, God still loves Israel, for He knew what they would be like. From the foundation of the world, he had prepared for this. He sent His only begotten Son into the world. "He came unto His own and His own received Him not," but that's alright because from a child Jesus knew that He "must be about His Father's business" of preaching, teaching, healing, and saving of souls. Because of their rejection of Him, Jesus taught in parables. He said in Luke 8:10, "The ones that I have chosen unto them is given the mysteries of the Kingdom of God, but to others in parables that seeing they might not see, and hearing they might not understand." So, Jesus turned to the Gentiles as a light. Paul had us to know in Romans 11:16-24 that we as Gentiles have nothing to brag about because Jesus turned to the Gentiles. He had us to know that because some of the branches were broken off, we, being a wild olive tree, were grafted in among them and with them partake of the root that God can graft them back in again.

Yes, people, I found in my research in the Old Testament and in the New Testament that, with the exception of Psalm 80, all references to Israel as the vine indicate a degenerate state of God's people. There are many scriptures about vines and vineyards pointing out how unresponsive God's people are to God. Jesus addresses this issue in John 15:1 when He declares, "I am the true vine and my Father is the vinedresser." It is God Himself that does the digging and pruning. Un-pruned branches drain strength and energy from the plant. The goal of pruning is to gain a larger production of fruit. As branches on the vine, we are to bear fruit, much fruit, and more fruit. As branches we of ourselves cannot bear fruit; we must abide in the vine which is Jesus Christ.

Yes, my brothers and sisters let us not be any of those branches that are cut off. This does not refer to removing men from salvation, but to the separation of those whose belief is not true and who do not produce genuine Christian fruit. The fruitless branches are those who like Judas the betrayer, never really understood Christ's purpose nor committed themselves to Christ. Let us take inventory of ourselves, for Jesus has commanded us from the hour that we were saved, whether it was the first hour or the eleventh hour of our lives, to "Go into the vineyard and work and whatsoever is right, I will give."

People, we should not be afraid, shy, or timid because just as God has hedged and fenced the vineyard, which is the world, we as individuals who are saved are hedged about with a permanent hedge to protect us from the enemy who is Satan and all of his forces. The only way that Satan can harm us is by permission from God. Sometimes God permits Satan to buffet us around, but God told us in His Holy Word found in I Peter 4:12-13, "Beloved, think it not strange the fiery trial which is to test you, as though some strange thing happened unto you, But rejoice, inasmuch as you are partakers of Christ's sufferings, that when his glory shall be revealed, you may be glad also with exceeding joy." My friends, we ought to be happy when we are tried because God tries all who say they have faith in Him. He always has tried His people, and He always will. He always brings all of His people out victoriously if they have put their trust in Him; He brought out all of the patriarchs, and He will bring us out if we trust Him.

Yes, we, the saved, after our training period is over, are to go out into the entire world. Our work is soul winning, or, at least, it should be. But, the sad part is that some of us never get through the training period. We never get around to soul winning. We are too busy majoring in the politics of the church, the church building, music, social life or, as we call it, fellowship, new teaching methods, prophecy, separation from the world, and victorious living. All of these things are fine, but the major emphasis of every Christian ought to be the thing in which most of us minor, the business of winning the lost--one by one.

My friends, as laborers in God's vineyard, let us be careful how we work. It is not the quantity of work but the quality that counts. God, in His infinite wisdom, pointed out the ant to us. In Proverbs 6:6-7 He said, "Go to the ant, you sluggard; consider her ways, and be wise: Which having no guide, overseer, or ruler, provides her food in the summer, and gathered her food in the harvest." Hebrews 6:9 says, "For God is not unrighteous to forget your work and labor of love, which you have shown toward his name, in that you have ministered to the saints, and do minister." So, let us work until the day is done because pay day is coming. We want to be faithful until death so that we will receive that crown of life. This is for the work that we have done in God's vineyard. If we have not worked in the vineyard, we will end up in the harvest of the earth. As explained in Revelation 14:18-20, that is when God send His angels, the watchmen of the watchtower, to harvest, "[. . .] with a sharp sickle in their hands and gather the vine of the earth for her grapes are fully ripe. And will cast it into the great winepress of the wrath of God. And the winepress will be trodden outside the city, and blood will come out of the winepress of the fierceness and wrath of Almighty God."

Finally, let us gird up our loins, lace up our shoes, and get stepping for the Lord, for He said in Revelation 22:12-15, "I come quickly and my reward is with me, to give every man according as his work shall be. I am Alpha and Omega, the beginning and the end, the first and the last. Blessed are they that do his commandments that they may have right to the tree of life, and may enter in through the gates into the city. For outside are dogs, and sorcerers, and fornicators, and murderers, and idolaters, and whosoever loves and makes a lie." The reason they are outside is because of the hedge or wall that God has built around the city. He put the final seal on His Word in verses 20-21 with the last promise and the last prayer of the Bible: "He who testifies these things says, Surely, I come quickly. Amen (so be it). Even so, come, Lord Jesus." The grace of our Lord Jesus Christ be with you all. Amen.

PRESSING ON

Philippians 3:14

Philippians 3:14 - *I press toward the mark for the prize of the high calling of God in Christ Jesus.*

In my research I found out it was not easy to give a subject to this Philippian epistle. Some call it a missionary letter; some call the theme "Joy in Christ"; yet another said "Christian Experience". I will try to combine "Christian Experience" and "Joy in Christ"

We find that Paul is the writer of this Philippian epistle. He was born in Tarsus, a city of Cilicia. As a boy he learned a trade as was the custom in the training of all Jewish boys; he learned tent making. He was educated in the Jewish synagogue by parents and teachers who were strict Pharisees. In his early teens Saul went to Jerusalem where he was a student under Gamaliel, one of the most noted rabbis and teachers and a member of the Sanhedrin. As a youth Paul was zealous. Being exceedingly zealous he became one of the most violent opposes of the Christians. Saul was so zealous in his persecutions that he went to the Jewish authorities and asked to be appointed to hunt down the Christians in other cities.

Saul left for Damascus "breathing out threatening and slaughter." Along the way he met a man John called Jesus. His name was changed from Saul to Brother Paul. He stopped sending people to the undertaker and started introducing them to the *upper*taker. After Paul's encounter with Jesus, Paul was blind for three days. He later said that it was that he might become a personal witness and an apostle, (Acts 9:1-8; 22:5-11; 26:12-18). As a new Christian, Paul did not become a successful preacher and missionary overnight, for he remained in and near Damascus for two years. He taught Christ so boldly that the Jews determined to kill him. Paul left Damascus going other places preaching Christ and Him crucified as well as establishing churches.

So, we find that the Philippian letter was written to the church at Philippi. This church had been established by the apostle Paul on his second missionary journey. The reason that Paul had gone to Philippi was because of a vision. Acts 16:9 says, "And a vision appeared to Paul in the night; There stood a man of Macedonia, and prayed him saying, Come over into Macedonia and help us." At the time of the writing of the letter, Paul was in prison in Rome. Epaphroditus came to visit him bringing an offering of money. Paul wrote this letter in gratitude and sent it back to the Philippians by Epaproditus. Paul addressed this letter "to all the saints in Christ Jesus who are at Philippi with the bishops and deacons." He is giving thanks to God for the Philippian church and for the fellowship that they had had in the gospel. He is telling them about the unhappiness and troubles there are in the world. Yet, he tells them to rejoice in the Lord always.

My friends, in Paul's Christian experiences he found out this one thing, "Be not deceived, God is not mocked (counterfeited) for whatsoever a man sows that shall he also reap" (Galatians 6:7). Even Job knew this, for he said in Job 4:8, "They that plow iniquity, and sow wickedness, reap the same." So, we find in II Corinthians 11:23-27 Paul recounts his suffering for the gospel. First, of the Jews five times he had received thirty-nine stripes, three times beaten with rods, and stoned once. He had also been shipwrecked three times, even spent 24 hours in the water. On many of his journeys he had been in danger from floods, robbers, both Jews and Gentiles, and many other perils. In spite of all these things, Paul thanks Christ Jesus our Lord, who had enabled him, counting him worthy to be in the ministry.

Yes, we find in Paul's Christian experiences that he was determined not to know anything among the people except Jesus Christ and him crucified and admonished them to also, "Let this mind be in you, which was also in Christ Jesus." If we have Jesus in our minds and on our minds then we know that God shall supply all our needs. Knowing this, ask yourself this question, "What shall separate us from the love of Christ?" Paul had matured enough to know that "for me to live is Christ, to die is gain."

He also knew that "If our earthly house of this tabernacle were dissolved, we have a building of God, an house not made with hands, eternal in the heavens" (II Cor. 5:1). For the cause of Christ, Paul didn't mind dying. In Acts 21:13 he said, "I am ready not to be bound only but also to die at Jerusalem for the name of Jesus Christ." Not only that but he also said in II Timothy 1:12, "For this cause I also suffered these things: nevertheless I am not ashamed: for I know whom I have believed, and am persuaded that he is able to keep that which I have committed unto him against that day."

Yes, in Paul's Christian experiences he was sometimes up and sometimes down, but through it all he said, "I know how to be abased, and I know how to abound; everywhere and in all things. I am instructed both to be full and to be hungry, both to abound and suffer need. I can do all things through Christ, who strengthened me" (Phil. 4:12-13). Yes, my friends, Paul had decided to run on and see what the end would be. He had been running for Jesus a long time, and he tells us in I Corinthians 9:24, "Know you not that they who run in a race run all, but one receives the prize? So run that you may obtain."

What are the benefits gotten from running? Even in the natural sense there are benefits derived from running. Take a jogger for instance; whether he is jogging in place, jogging around the block, or a mile or two, he gets benefits. Before he starts jogging, some preparations must be made. He must have on the proper clothing and shoes; these enable him to run faster and smoother. Even so, in the spiritual sense some preparations must be made. We must be properly clothed. As described in Ephesians 6:11-18, we must have on the whole armor of God that we may be able to run in the race. We must have truth as a belt, tight around our waist, righteousness as our breastplate, our shoes, the gospel of peace, and at all times we must carry faith as a shield, take salvation as a helmet, and the word of God as a sword, which the Spirit gives us. Do all of this in prayer, asking for God's help. Then, and only then, are we ready to run in the race.

Now that we are ready to run in the race, let's get back to the benefits. What are the benefits? In the natural sense the jogger gets muscle tone, stamina, weight loss, good heart beat, endurance, and just plain good feeling. Did you not know that running in the Christian race also has benefits? First you get muscle tone which enables you to fight sin and Satan. Stamina enables you to stand when you just can't, but you stand anyway. You lose weight when you shed "the weight and the sin that so easily beset you" and lets you run with patience. Good heart beat happens when you love those that despitefully use you and say all manner of evil about you. Endurance is just a natural benefit when you "endure hardness as a good soldier of Christ." You get a good feeling when you learn how to, "Forget those things which are behind, and reaching forth unto those things which are before" (Phil. 3:13b). And, as our theme scripture says, we can "press (get in a hurry) toward (on foot) the mark (the goal) for the prize (the reward) of the high calling (divine summons) of God in Christ Jesus." Yes, my friends, let us run on in the race, straining every nerve and muscle, exerting every ounce of strength like the jogger. But, if you can't jog, a fast walk will do lest we come short of the goal. Know that in this race, God will stand by you; He is the way and the truth that is the path to walk or run in and the light of the world that lights your path, so the race is fixed; you can't fail if you start.

So, pray on; don't stop. Sing on; don't stop. Preach on; don't stop, and run on; don't stop. Then at last we can say just like Paul, "For I am now ready to be offered, and the time of my departure is at hand. I have fought a good fight; I have finished my course (meaning the race); I have kept the faith (you can do nothing without faith). Henceforth there is laid up for me a crown of righteousness, which the Lord, the righteous judge, shall give me at that day: and not to me only, but unto all them that love his appearing," (II Timothy 4:6-8).

Finally, my friends, the good feeling that we have comes from that benefit of joy. Jesus came to bring us tidings of great joy. He told us in John 15:11, "These things have I spoken unto you, that my joy might remain in you, and that your joy might be full." John 16:22 says, "Your heart shall rejoice and your joy no man takes from you." People, this joy that I have the world didn't give it, and the world can't take it away. If you don't have joy, maybe you are not in the race or not running properly or not pressing on. Read the instruction manual, those 66 books, for the plan.

"Now the God of peace, that brought again from the dead our Lord Jesus, that great shepherd of the sheep, through the blood of the everlasting covenant make you perfect in every good work to do his will (or run the race) working in you that which is well pleasing in his sight through Jesus Christ, to whom be glory forever and ever. Amen" (Hebrews 13:20-21).

CALLING, HEARING,
AND ANSWERING

II Chronicles 7:14

II Chronicles 7:14 - *If my people which are called by my name, shall humble themselves, and pray, and seek my face, and turn from their wicked ways; then will I hear from heaven, and will forgive their sin, and will heal their land.*

The writer of II Chronicles has been ascribed by some to be Ezra; others say Author Unknown. The two books of Chronicles are largely a retelling of events recorded in the books of Samuel and Kings but from a different point of view. II Chronicles describes the rule of King Solomon and records the revolt of the northern tribes led by Jeroboam against Rehoboam, Solomon's sons and successors. The book continues an account of the history of the Kingdom of Judah until the fall of Jerusalem.

So, we read in II Chronicles 7:14, "If my people which are called by my name, shall humble themselves, and pray, and seek my face, and turn from their wicked ways; then will I hear from heaven, and will forgive their sin, and will heal their land. Notice, God told them four things to do. The numerical principle (Hermeneutics) could be applied here, for there is a spiritual meaning and significance behind this number "four." In brief, number four is the creation number. It has special reference to the earth ("heal their land"). If we study the Scripture, we will find a lot of references to the number four. For instance, when the Lord Jesus gave his discourse on the Mount of Olives about events which should transpire and precede His return, He spoke to only four: Peter, James, John, and Andrew.

Let's move on. This scripture is a promise that God made to Solomon concerning His people, Israel, at the dedication of the temple. Note, Israel is called His people. Is this just for Israel? What about us? As believers in Christ, we become God's sons through faith in Jesus Christ. So, as sons of God in union with Christ, this same promise can be applied to us today. In this scripture is found the formula for successful Christian living. When all of the ingredients have been put together, it places us in compliance to the will of God. In our natural lives if we are going to do a specific thing, we check to see if we have all of the parts or all of the ingredients to do what we plan. If we don't have everything needed, we add it, or we go and get the necessary things. So, it is the same in our spiritual lives.

Let's look at the ingredients; let us see what God is saying. First He said to "humble" yourself. The word "humble" means not proud, to be meek. Well, how can you humble yourself? Colossians 3:12 tells us, "Put on therefore, as the elect of God, holy and beloved, bowels of mercies, kindness, humbleness of mind, meekness, longsuffering." Not only should we put on, but be clothed with humility, "For God resists the proud, and gives grace to the humble" (I Peter 5:5). So, we see that to be humble is necessary for the service of God.

Secondly, God said to "pray". The word "pray" means to entreat, implore, or petition. How do you pray? One method of prayer has been described as bowing the knees (Ephesians 3:14), looking up (Psalm 5:13), lifting up the heart (Lamentations 3:41), pouring out our soul (I Samuel 1:15), and calling upon the name of the Lord (Genesis 12:8; Psalm 116:4; Acts 22:16). Prayer should be offered up in faith (Matthew 21:22; Hebrews 11:6; James 1:6), with a true heart, and a desire to be heard and answered. We should even have a time to pray. Psalm 55:17 says, "Evening, and morning, and at noon, will I pray, and cry aloud: And he shall hear my voice."

The third thing God said was to "seek". The word "seek" means search for, try to find. Well, how do we seek God? The answer is through prayer, for Isaiah 55:6 says, "Seek the Lord while he may be found, call upon him while he is near." Matthew 7:7 says, "Ask, and it shall be given you; seek, and you shall find; knock, and it shall be opened unto you."

The fourth and final thing God said was to "turn from your wicked ways." How can this be done? This is done by faith, taking God at His word. Acts 11:21 tells us, "And the hand of the Lord was with them; and a great number believed and turned unto the Lord." In Romans 4:5 the person who depends on his faith, not on his deeds, and who believes in the God who declares the guilty to be innocent, it is his faith that God takes into account in order to put him right with himself.

So, we find that humbleness, prayerfulness, and seeking will not do unless we turn from our wicked ways. We need all of the ingredients in the formula in order to do what God wants us to do. Our church choir used to sing a song by James Cleveland that tells us to do what God wants us to do, "try to do our best, try to stand the test." Be willing to "go through the storm and rain; try hard not to complain." We should let our "little light shine; some lost sheep's bound to find." In essence do God's will.

Yes, people, do God's will. The promises that God makes are sure, and we can be fully assured that He will keep them because Hebrews 6:18-19 says, "That by two immutable things in which it was impossible for to lie, we might have a strong consolation, who have fled for refuge to lay hold upon the hope set before us: Which hope we have as an anchor of the soul, both sure and steadfast, and goes through the curtain of the heavenly temple into the inner sanctuary."

My friends, as believers in God, it's not an easy road. God has told us in His word that all who live godly shall suffer persecution, "But let none of you suffer as a murderer, or a thief, or as an evil doer, or as a busybody in other people's business" (I Peter 4:15). Let us cast off former sinful habits and walk in the newness of life. That path will be easier if we know, reckon, and yield. We should know " That our old man is crucified with him, that the body of sin might be destroyed, that henceforth we should not serve sin" (Romans 6:6); we should "Likewise reckon also yourselves to be dead indeed unto sin, but alive unto God through Jesus Christ our Lord" (vs. 11), and we should "Neither yield your members as instruments of unrighteousness unto sin: but yield yourselves unto God, as those that are alive from the dead, and your members as instruments of righteousness unto God" (vs.13).

Yes, if we do these things as we walk this road to glory, we can say like that old song:

"Beams of heaven as I go through this wilderness below, / Guide my feet in peaceful ways; turn my midnight into day." We can also look to the hills from whence comes our help (Psalm 121:1), praise God from whom all blessings flow as we hold to God's unchanging hand, and keep looking for a miracle because God will take care of you. You know what? I've got a feeling that every thing is going to be alright because He's that kind of friend.

Yes, my friends, if God's promises were good enough for Israel, they are good enough for me. Yes, along the way in this life, I think of the words of another song that I want to share with you: "We are our heavenly Fathers children, and we know that He loves us one and all." In spite of our shortcomings, God still loves us because "He knows, yes, He knows just how much we can bear." Sometimes we seek answers to problems from friends and loved ones; we seem to forget that "There is a God that rules earth and heaven;" and he has the care or relief from "every pain or care, And He knows, yes, He knows Just how much we can bear."

So, we ought to be happy knowing that whether we live, as one song says, "In a mansion made of stone, or in a shanty all alone, God cares." As we go through this life "Calling, Hearing, and Answering", sometimes think of the words of a poem, "A Bend in the Road":

When we feel we have nothing left to give, and we are sure that the song has ended.
When our day seems over and the shadows fall, and the darkness of night has descended,
Where can we go to find the strength to keep on trying?
Where can we find the hand that will dry the tears that the heart is crying?

There's but one place to go and that is to God, dropping all pretense and pride.
We can pour out our problems without restraint and gain strength with Him at our side,
And together we stand at life's crossroads and view what we think is the end,
But God has a bigger vision, and He tells us it's only a Bend.

For the road goes on and is smoother and the "pause in the song" is a rest.
And the part that's unsung and unfinished is the sweetest and richest and best.
So rest and relax and grow stronger; Let go and let God share your load.
Your work is not finished or ended; you've just come to "A Bend in the Road".

REMOVING SPOTS AND IRONING OUT WRINKLES

Ephesians 5:27

Ephesians 5:27 - *That he might present it to himself a glorious church, not having spot, or wrinkle, or any such thing; but that it should be holy and without blemish.*

The scripture for this theme is found in Ephesians. This letter was written by the apostle Paul to the church at Ephesus. He is concerned first of all with God's plan-- to bring all creation together, everything in heaven and on earth, with Christ as the head. It is also an appeal to God's people to live out the meaning of this great plan for the unity of mankind through oneness with Jesus Christ.

Several figures of speech are used to show the oneness of God's people in union with Christ. First, the church is like a body with Christ as the head, second, like a building with Christ as the cornerstone, and third, like a wife with Christ as the husband. In this letter the writer is moved by the thought of God's grace in Christ. Everything is seen in the light of Christ's love, sacrifice, forgiveness, grace, and purity. So, we read in Ephesians 5:27, "That he might present it to himself a glorious church, not having spot, or wrinkle, or any such thing; but that it should be holy and without blemish."

The issue is: removing spots and ironing out wrinkles. The question is: How can it be done? In order to find the answer to the question, we have to go back to the Alpha and Omega, the beginning and the end, the first and the last, the which is, the which was, and the which is to come, the Almighty God (Rev.1:8, 22:13). Abraham Lincoln said in his Gettysburg address: "Four score and seven years ago, our forefathers brought forth on this continent a new nation conceived in liberty and dedicated to the proposition that all men are created equal." I say that thousands of years ago, the great God of the universe, brought forth on this planet a plan conceived in liberty and dedicated to the proposition that all men are created in his likeness and image.

Thus God created them male and female (Genesis 1:27), made them a little lower than the angels, crowned them with glory and honor, made them to have dominion over the works of His hands, and put all things under their feet (Psalm 8:5-6). The man that God created He named Adam, a Hebrew word meaning mankind, translated as a proper name to represent the father of the human race. The woman, Adam named Eve. The term personifies life; the name means the mother of all living (Gen.2:18-4:2). Adam and Eve were perfect in every way. They were to work together in unison as one, and indeed they did until along came the serpent, that old devil.

We find that things worked out alright until the devil appeared. Yes, they were fine until they got to talking around with the serpent. Instead of obeying God, they obeyed the devil, and they found out the penalty for disobeying God. They had eaten of the forbidden fruit; things changed. In shame they hung their heads. On that day, as a result of their sin of disobedience to God, by the one man Adam death came.

Also, on the same day that sin brought death, God promised a Savior. In *The Good News Bible* Genesis 3:15 says, "I will make you (the serpent, or the devil) and the woman hate each other; her offspring and yours will always be enemies. Her offspring will crush your head, and you will bite their heel." I Corinthians 15:22 tells us, "For as in Adam all die, even so in Christ shall all be made alive." We find that God had to change His plans. Where there had been only good, now, there was evil. Where there was perfection, there is now imperfection. Where there was unity, now there is separation. Where there was love, now, there is hatred. If we read I Corinthians 15:46-47, it says, "Howbeit that was not first which is spiritual, but that which is natural; and afterward that which is spiritual. The first man is of the earth, earthy: the second man is the Lord from heaven." In I Corinthians 15:45, "[. . .] the first man Adam was made a living soul; the last man Adam was made a quickening spirit." Both men were God's sons, the first of the earth and the second of the spirit. The end of the genealogy in Luke 3:48, reads, "Which was the son of Enos, which was the son of Seth, which was the son of Adam, which was the son of God." In Luke 3:22, "And the Holy Ghost descended in a bodily shape like a dove upon him, and a voice came from heaven, which said, You are my beloved Son; in you I am well pleased."

When Jesus was teaching and preaching, He used the natural to illustrate the Spiritual. I will try to do the same with the revelations that God has given me by the aid of the Holy Spirit. I was lead to the scripture in Ecclesiastes 1:9-11 where the preacher said, "The thing that has been, it is that which shall be; and that which is done is that which shall be done: and there is no new thing under the sun. Is there anything whereof it may be said, See, this is new? It has been already of old time, which was before us. There is no remembrance of former things; neither shall there be any remembrance of things that are to come with those that shall come after." I will try to show you tonight just what he was talking about. The issue remains: removing spots and ironing out wrinkles. The question is: "How can it be done?"

Well, let us continue on in our discourse. Let us go back to the beginning. A lot of people say that the church came into existence after the Day of Pentecost. I'm here to tell you that the church always has been and always will be. The church belongs to God, and it is the body of Christ, and Christ is the head. I Timothy 3:15 tells us, "But if I tarry long, that you may know how you ought to behave yourself in the house of God, which is the church of the living God, the pillar and ground of truth." Colossians 1:18 reads, "And he is the head of the body, the church: who is the beginning. He is the first born son, who was raised from death, in order that he alone might have the first place in all things." So, the church has always been in existence, even in the creation, for Genesis 1:26 says, "And God said, Let us make man;" this was the first man Adam, and there was the second man Adam, Christ, who was also there in the beginning.

My sisters and my brothers, Christ has been called many names and titles, and Adam (I Cor. 15:45) was just one of them. Just to name a few, He was also called Almighty (Revelation 1:18), Amen (3:14), Alpha and Omega (1:18; 22:13), Bread of Life (John 6:35, 48), Chief Cornerstone (Ephesians 2:20; I Peter 2:6), Head of the Church (Eph. 5:23; Col. 1:18), Rock (I Cor. 10:4), and Husband of the Church (Isaiah 54:5-6; Eph. 5:25-32; Isa. 62:5; Rev. 21:2,9).

Of all of the names and titles of Christ, I would like to speak about the Head, the Stone or the Rock, and Husband of the church. The Biblical meaning of the word "head" is part of the body or place of honor. *Webster's Dictionary* definition is the upper or anterior division of the body that contains the brain, the chief sense organs, or the mouth. We find that the head is the most important part of the body; without the head there would be no life. If you want to kill a person or mess them up real bad, start at the head. You can cut off a hand, foot, leg, or arm, and the part cut off will die unless it is surgically reattached to the body. The body will continue to operate with or without it, but if you cut off the head, the body will die.

In the spiritual sense, Christ is the head of the church which is his body. We, as Christians, are parts or members of Christ's body. If we get cut off from the body, we will die; we are only members of the body. The body, which is Christ, will continue to operate. John 1:4 tell us, "In him was life and the life was the light of men." Jesus said, "I am the resurrection and the life" (John 11:25). Without Christ, the Head, we could not exist. As believers in Christ, we should be careful about to what we join our bodies. To whatever we are joined, we become one. If we are joined to Christ, we are one. If we are joined to a sinner, we are one. Romans 12:1 tells us, "I beseech you therefore, brethren, by the mercies of God, that you present your bodies a living sacrifice, holy, acceptable unto God, which is your reasonable service."

Aside from being called the Head of the Church, Christ was called Rock and Stone. The Biblical meaning of rock is a concreted mass of stony material; a cliff or crag. It might serve as a dwelling or a place of refuge, strength, and security. A stone is a piece of detached rock, rock slabs, or blocks used especially for building material. Stones were used to block the entrance to caves and sepulchers; they were also used in slings and hurled as missiles. Boundary marks and scale weights were normally stone. Stones were heaped as use in memorials. Stone was used as the Hebrew legal mode of death.

Since Christ was called Stone and Rock, I would like to talk about the Stone first, and remember that the preacher said, "There is nothing new under the sun. The thing that has been, is that which shall be, and that which is done, is that which shall be done." Now, let us take Jacob, for instance. In Genesis 28:10-18 Jacob found out about the Stone while he was going to his Uncle Laban's house to get a wife as his father had instructed him to do. "As he journeyed along, he came to a certain place and camped there. He lay down to sleep, resting his head on a <u>stone</u>. He dreamed that he saw a ladder reaching from earth to heaven with angels going up and down on it" (vs. 11-12). Verses 13-15 continue the story, "And there was the Lord standing beside him saying, I am the Lord, the God of Abraham and Isaac. I will give to you and your descendants this land on which you are lying. They will be as numerous as the specks of dust on the earth. They will extend their territory in all directions, and through you and all your descendants I will bless all the nations. Remember I will be with you and protect you wherever you go, and I will bring you back to this land. I will not leave you until I have done all that I have promised you." The story continues with, "Jacob woke up and said the Lord is here! He is in this place, and I didn't know it! He was afraid and said what a terrifying place this is! It must be the house of God; it must be the gate that opens into heaven. Jacob got up early the next morning, took the <u>stone</u> that was under his head, and set it up for a pillar, and poured oil upon the top of it" (vs. 16-18). This natural stone gained a spiritual representation; remember the natural is first then the spiritual.

The spiritual nature of the anointing of the stone reminds me of the anointing of Jesus, the Stone, before and after His crucifixion. The stone plays an important role in the story of the resurrection of Jesus as told in Matthew 28:1-7. Mary Magdalene and the other Mary were at the sepulcher. "There was a great earthquake: for the angel of the Lord descended from heaven, and came and rolled back the stone from the door, and sat on it" (28:2). The guards were afraid, and became as dead men. The angel talked with the women and told them, "[. . .] he goes before you into Galilee" (vs.7). As they were leaving, "Jesus appeared unto them, and they worshipped him." Jesus told them, "[. . .] go tell my brethren to go into Galilee and there you will see me" (vs.10). Later, the disciples went to Galilee, and Jesus appeared unto them. Jesus commissioned them saying, "Go, therefore, and teach all nations, baptizing them in the name of the Father, and of the Son, and of the Holy Ghost: Teaching them to observe all things whatsoever I have commanded you and, lo, I am with you always, even unto the end of the world" (vs. 19-20).

Let's continue with Jacob and the natural use of the stone. Jacob's journey continues in the 29th chapter. "Jacob continued on his way until he came into the land of the east. He looked and saw a well in the field, and there were three flocks of sheep lying by it; for out of that well they watered the flocks: and a great <u>stone</u> was upon the well's mouth" (vs.1-2).

The story continues as,"Jacob asked the shepherds where they were from, and they said from Haran. Well, do you know Laban the son of Nahor? They said, yes we do. Jacob asked them was he (Laban) well; they said Yes, and here comes his daughter Rachel with his flock, it was about noon" (vs. 4-7). Verse 9 continues, "While Jacob was still talking with them, Rachel arrived with the flock. When Jacob saw Rachel with his uncle Laban's flock, he went to the well, <u>rolled the stone back</u>, and watered the sheep. Then he kissed her and began to cry for joy. He told her, I am your father's relative, the son of Rebecca. She ran to tell her father.

Doesn't this remind you of the story of Jesus and the woman at the well. John 4:3-29 records the story. Jesus left Judea and went back to Galilee; on his way there he had to go through Samaria. In Samaria he came to a town named Sychar which was not far from the field that Jacob had given his son Joseph. Jacob's well was there, and Jesus, the Stone, (the spiritual stone) tired out by the trip, sat on the well (Jacob's well), and it was about the sixth hour (noon). There came a Samaritan woman to draw some water, and Jesus said to her, "Give me a drink of water." Jesus and the woman had a conversation. When Jesus got through talking with her, "The woman left her water pot, and went into the city and said to the men, come, see a man [. . .]" (vs. 28-29a). Both Rachel and the Samaritan woman ran to tell about a man they had met; Rachel's man was natural, but the Samaritan's man was spiritual. Remember, the preacher said, "There is nothing new under the sun. The thing that has been (in Genesis), is that which shall be (in John), and that which is done (in Genesis), is that which shall be done (in John)." The natural occurrence in Genesis was a foreshadowing of the spiritual occurrence in John.

David also knew about the Stone, for as he prepared to go in to fight Goliath the giant, he chose five smooth <u>stones</u> and put them in his shepherd's bag. Notice, they were five *smooth stones*, no wrinkles, but smooth, even stones. Now, let us pause to analyze this. First, David chose the stones; now God, the Stone, chooses us. Secondly, there were smooth stones just as we should have no spots or wrinkles, smooth. Thirdly, David was experienced in using stones, for he knew that a smooth stone would penetrate into what it is hurled at. So are we, as lively stones, able to penetrate the lives of others when we become experienced in the usage of God's word. We can be powerful witnesses if we just use the penetrating power of God's word. David went out to fight the giant. Goliath had a sword, a spear, and a shield; David had the stone. David stepped out in the name of the Lord, and he might have said, "I will lift up mine eyes unto the hills from whence comes my help. My help comes from the Lord, which made heaven and earth" (Psalm 121:1). David hurled the stone that smooth stone; it penetrated the giant's head. The stone won the battle.

I imagine the Stone, Jesus, probably told Satan, "I don't care how big your kingdom gets; I'm going to tear it down." So, I challenge you as I Peter 2:4-6, "Come to the Lord, the living stone rejected by man, but chosen of God, and precious. Come as living stones and let yourselves be used in building the spiritual temple, where you will serve as holy priests to offer spiritual and acceptable sacrifices to God through Jesus Christ." The scripture continues with," Behold, I lay in Zion a chief corner stone, elect, precious, and whoever believes in him will never be disappointed."

Now, fellow stones, you lively stones, let us look at the rock. Rock has many uses. In olden days it was used to wash with. My son, Joseph, told me that in Korea they still wash clothes on the rock. We drink water from the rock; you usually see pictures of fresh water running over rock. Animals make homes and birds make nests in the rock. Moses was well acquainted with the rock; he smote the rock. Later he was told to speak to the rock, but he disobeyed and smote the rock twice (Numbers 20:8). Jesus, the Rock would only be smitten once, not twice, for all, through the crucifixion (Romans 6:10; I Peter 4:18). All we have to do is speak to the Rock; we can "come boldly before the throne of grace" (Hebrews 4:16). Moses did not know at that time that living water came out of the Rock. But, in Deuteronomy 32:4 Moses said, "He (God) is the Rock, his work is perfect: for all his ways are judgment; a God of truth and without iniquity; just and right is he." In I Samuel 2:2 Hannah praised God in her prayer saying, "There is none holy as the Lord: for there is none beside you; neither is there any rock like our God. David said in his song of deliverance, after being delivered from all of his enemies, including King Saul, in II Samuel 22:2, "The Lord is my rock, and my fortress, and my deliverer;" in verse 32, "For who is God, save the Lord: And who is a rock, save our God; and verse 47, "The Lord lives: and blessed be my rock; and exalted be the God of the rock of my salvation. Yes, sisters and brothers, you ought to get a piece of the Rock. Oh, my Jesus is a rock in a weary land, a shelter in the time of a storm.

Jesus has also been called the Husband of the Church. The Biblical meaning of the word "husband" is head of household. On the natural side, as head of the household, a man's duty is to love, honor, and cherish his wife in sickness and in health. His is also to bring up the children in the nurture and admonition of the Lord. These are the duties of a Christian husband. Spiritually, as head of the household of God, Christ loved the church and gave himself for it. John 3:16 tells us, "For God so loved the world, that He gave His only begotten son, that whosoever believeth in him should not perish, but have everlasting life." Furthermore, as head of the household, a husband is to have a home for his wife and children. Jesus told us in John 14:1-3, "Do not be worried and upset, Believe in God and also believe in me. In my Father's house are many mansions (not cribs, shanties or shacks) if it were not so, I would have told you. I go to prepare a place for you, and If I go and prepare a place for you, I will come again, and receive you unto myself; that where I am there you may be also."

The issue was removing spots and ironing out wrinkles. The question still remains: How can it be done? Ephesians 5:23-27 tells us, "For the husband is the head of the wife, even as Christ is the head of the Church: And Christ is himself the savior of the church, his body. Therefore, as the church is subject unto Christ, so let the wives be to their own husbands in everything. Husbands, love your wives, even as Christ loved the Church and gave himself for it: That he might sanctify and cleanse it with the washing of water by the word, That he might present it to himself a glorious church, not having spot or wrinkle, or any such thing; but that it should be holy and without blemish."

Since this issue is a Christian issue concerning the church, we need to know that we are chosen by God, and we ought to be glad, for he said in Romans 9:15, "I will have mercy on whom I will have mercy, and compassion on whom I will have compassion." Isaiah 44:7 says, "I form the light, and create darkness: I make peace, and create evil: I the Lord do all these things." Thus, God set the method for removing spots and ironing out wrinkles. Jesus is the only one who can remove spots and iron out wrinkles in our lives. He is the Stone or Rock who cleanses us by washing us with the living water. Wrinkles usually require ironing which is heat which we will call love. As a husband He shows us love by feeding us the living bread, by clothing us in righteousness, by sheltering us in his arms, by keeping us in sanctification, by holding us in his hands, by walking with us by night and by day, by loving us as himself, and, of course, by giving Himself for us on the cross. Jesus is the greatest spot and wrinkle remover that I know; He has the remedy for all. Brothers and sisters, you get a piece of the Rock, marry it, and live happily ever after.

Written by Mary Hampton Battle and Edited by Edna Yvonne James

"Now unto him that is able to keep you from falling, and to present you faultless (spotless and wrinkle free) before the presence of his glory with exceeding joy, To the only wise God our savior, be glory and majesty, dominion and power, both now and ever. Amen" (Jude 24-25).

OUR MISSION FOR CHRIST

Matthew 28:19-20

Matthew 28:19-20 - *Go therefore, and teach all nations baptizing them in the name of the Father, and of the Son, and of the Holy Ghost: Teaching them to observe all things whatsoever I have commanded you: and lo, I am with you always, even unto the end of the world.*

The scripture is found in the gospel according to Matthew. It tells the good news that Jesus is the promised Savior, the one through whom God fulfilled the promises he made to his people in the Old Testament. This good news was not only for the Jewish people, among whom Jesus was born and lived, but for the whole world. The book of Matthew is carefully arranged. It begins with the birth of Jesus, describes his baptism and temptation, then takes up his ministry of preaching, teaching, and healing. After this the gospel records His journey from Galilee to Jerusalem and His last week ending in His crucifixion and resurrection.

In Matthew Chapter 28 are recorded the events leading up to Jesus giving the Great Commission, on which the theme is based, to the eleven disciples. In these verses is one of the greatest missionary appeals that we find in the entire Bible: "Go therefore, and teach all nations baptizing them in the name of the Father, and of the Son, and of the Holy Ghost: Teaching them to observe all things whatsoever I have commanded you; and lo, I am with you always, even unto the end of the world." The theme is "Our Mission for Christ."

We have heard the story about the death, burial, and resurrection of Jesus. His resurrection was early one Sunday morning which was the first day of the week. Mary Magdalene and other women had bought sweet spices so that they might come and anoint his body. As they were on their way to the burial place, they wondered who would roll away the stone from the door of the sepulcher. But, I tell you, God knows our hearts, and He knows our thoughts because when they got there the stone was rolled away. Upon entering the sepulcher, they saw an angel sitting on the right side dressed in a long white garment, and they were frightened. The angel told them, "Fear not, for I know that you seek Jesus, which was crucified. He is not here; for he is risen as he said." We have here a testimony that you can't explain away, lie away, or ignore, and that is the resurrection. Jesus had told his disciples before He was crucified that He would rise the third day. This testimony will remain forever; nothing can destroy this truth. The tomb was empty, and Christ was responsible for it.

Yet, we are not nearly as interested in the angel, the earthquake, or even the women of this story, as we are in the fact declared: "He is not here, for he is risen as he said. Come see the place where the Lord lay." I don't know how these women felt when they did what the angel said, but I am sure of this: when they did see the empty tomb, they were ready to go and tell. Yes, it was quite an experience for these women seeing the stone rolled away, the empty tomb, and an angel that sat and talked with them telling them to go. They went out quickly, afraid, yet filled with joy, to tell the disciples the good news. As they were on their way to tell the disciples the good news, lo and behold they met Jesus. Tell me how would you feel if you had found that empty burial place, and then a little later meet the person that had occupied it? How much can you stand! All of this was happening in one day. Yes, Jesus made a number of post resurrection appearances, but this was the first. Jesus greeted the women bidding them not to fear; they fell at His feet and worshipped him. Again He repeated the missionary plea: "Go and tell."

My friends, Jesus not only appeared to these women but He also was seen by Cleopas and Simon as they were going to a village called Emmaeus. As they walked, they talked about all of the things that had been happening. As they were walking along, Jesus himself drew near and walked along with them. They saw him but did not recognize him. Jesus asked them what they were talking about. They stood with sad faces and told him all of the things that had happened concerning Jesus. How that

Jesus was a prophet and had been sentenced to death and crucified and how the women had not found his body. Then Jesus said to them, "How foolish you are, and how slow you are to believe everything the prophets said, was it not necessary for the Messiah to suffer these things and then to enter his glory?" (Luke 24:25-26). Then Jesus explained to them what was said about him in all the Scriptures beginning with the book of Moses and the writings of all the prophets. Later, after they had recognized who Jesus was, "They said one to another; Did not our heart burn within us, while he talked with us by the way, while he opened to us the scriptures?" (vs. 32). Yes, you will have the heart burn every time you have a personal encounter with Jesus; just a little talk with Jesus makes it all alright.

So, we see the number of witnesses of the resurrection mounting. First, it was the Angel at the grave, then the women, the guards that were on duty, Cleopas, and Simon. All of these bore witness to the fact that the Son of God was no longer in the tomb of Joseph; He was risen. Jesus was seen by all of these witnesses plus the eleven disciples, and for forty days after His resurrection, He appeared to them many times in ways that proved beyond a doubt that He was alive. On one occasion when the disciples saw him, He talked with them about the Kingdom. On another occasion when they came together, He gave them this order: "Do not leave Jerusalem but wait for the promise of the Father" (Acts 1:4). It was during this time that Jesus gave the last instructions to his disciples. Friends, I have always been interested in people's last words. The last thing my father said to me and others before he died was, "If I don't see you anymore, everything is alright between me and God."

So, here we have the resurrected King speaking his last words to His people giving to them what is called The Great Commission. It was given to the eleven who were with Him then, and it is also given to the church today. It is a commission backed up by all authority. Matthew 28:18 tells us, "All power (authority) is given unto me in heaven and in earth." Verse 19 then says, "Go therefore, and teach all nations, baptizing them in the name of the Father, and of the Son, and of the Holy Ghost." This Great Commission, which is founded upon the power and glory of Christ, is a commission to all of us to go and tell the message. It was to be given to all nations thus enabling both Jews and Gentiles to become disciples of the King.

In the Great Commission the disciples were told to teach. Being converted and baptized will not fully equip a person for service. Too often our churches fail at this point. The commission tells us that following conversion and baptism there is to be education. You don't educate a person into being saved, but you educate a saved person. What were the disciples to teach? Verse 20 says, "[. . .] teaching them to observe all things whatsoever I have commanded you." What Christ is saying here is to teach new converts the whole word of God not the tradition of men or philosophy but the Word.

Along with this commission there is a precious promise, "[. . .] lo, I am with you always, even unto the end of the world." Jesus is telling us that He will never fail you regardless of how dark or difficult the day may be. With this promise in mind, it should encourage each of us as Christians to be on our mission for Christ: observing and teaching all that He commanded. We should be ready to go into the vineyard and work and "whatsoever is right" will be our pay. We should be ready like Peter was in John 21:15 when Jesus asked him, "Simon, son of Jonas, do you love me more than these? Simon answered; yea Lord you know that I love you. The Lord said unto him, Feed my lambs."

Friends, on our mission for Christ, it will not be easy, for Christ tells us in Matthew 7:13-15, "Go in through the narrow gate, because the gate to hell is wide and the road that leads to it is easy and there are many who travel it. But the gate to life is narrow and the way that leads to it is hard, and there are few people who find it. Be on your guard against false prophets; they come to you looking like sheep on the outside, but on the inside they are really like wild wolves. You will know them by what they do? (*The Good News Bible*). In Matthew 10:16 Jesus tells us, "I send you forth as sheep in the midst of wolves: be therefore wise as serpents and harmless as doves."

Yes, our mission for Christ is the same today as it was a long time ago in Bethany with the disciples. We must be fully equipped just as the disciples were, for Jesus tells us in Acts1:8, "But when the Holy Spirit comes upon you, you will be filled with power and you will be witnesses for me in Jerusalem, in all of Judea and Samaria, and to the ends of the earth." It is a must that we are filled with the power from on high in order to be efficient witnesses for Christ. Then we can go and tell the good news: how Christ died, was buried, and rose from the grave on our behalf. We can tell dying men, sinking women, girls, and boys that the wages of sin is death; the gift of God is eternal life. We can tell it and excel in it everywhere we go. We must look sharp, feel sharp, and be sharp, using the word of God correctly and having the Holy Ghost as our guide because we are on the battlefield, and we're working for Jesus. Yes, we're working for Jesus, and as we go about the business, let us love one another. "It wouldn't profit us anything if we could speak with the tongues of men and of angels and have not love. Our speech would sound like a noisy gong or a clanging bell. We may have the gift of inspired preaching, we may have all knowledge and understand all secrets: we may have all the faith needed to move mountains--but if we have no love, it is nothing" (I Cor. 13:1-2, paraphrased, *The Good News Bible)*. So, let us work in deeds and not just words. Let us put on the whole armor of God, and then we can say one to another, "You wear it well."

My brothers and my sisters, I want you to know that on my mission for Christ every second, every minute, every hour, every day, every week every month, through the years come what may, I feel like going on. The reason I feel this way is because I know what the end will be for those that overcome. To overcome means something. Listen to what I John 2:14 says, "I have written unto you, fathers, because you have known him that existed from the beginning. I have written unto you, young men, because you are strong, and the word of God abides in you, and you have overcome the wicked one." After overcoming, listen to the promises that Jesus made in Revelation 2:7, 11, 17, and 26. "He that has an ear, let him hear what the Spirit says unto the churches; To him that overcomes will I give to eat of the tree of life, which is in the midst of the paradise of God. [. . .] He that overcomes shall not be hurt of the second death (fire and brimstone). [. . .] To him that overcomes will I give to eat of the hidden manna, and will give him a white stone, and in the stone a new name written, which no man knows saving he that receives it. [. . .] He that overcomes and keeps my works unto the end, to him will I give power over the nations."

Revelation 3:5, 12, 21 continues with, "He that overcomes shall be clothed in white raiment; and I will not remove his name from the book of the living. In the presence of my Father and of his angels I will declare openly that they belong to me. [. . .] Him that overcomes I will make a pillar in the temple of my God, and he will never leave it; I will write on him the name of my God, and the name of the city of my God, the New Jerusalem, which will come down out of heaven from my God. I will also write on him my new name. [. . .] To him that overcomes will I grant to sit with me in my throne, even as I also overcome, and am set down with my Father in his throne." Then Revelation 21:7 says, "He that overcomes shall inherit all things; and I will be his God, and he shall be my son."

Yes, my brothers and my sisters, we shall overcome; yes, we shall overcome someday. I know we will because through the years we've kept on toiling, toiling through the storm and rain, hopefully, patiently working 'til the Savior comes again. But through it all what I love about being on my mission for Christ is like the words of a song: "I've seen the lightning flashing, and I've heard the thunder roll;" but through it all "I heard the voice of Jesus telling me still to fight on. He promised never to leave me . . . alone." Thank you.

JESUS: THE WAY, THE TRUTH, AND THE LIFE

John 14:6

John 14:6 - *Jesus said unto him, I am the way, the truth, and the life: no man comes unto the Father, but by me.*

This scripture is found in one of the Gospels. The Gospel reveals Christ to us that we may believe and want to become Christians. According to the Gospel of St. John, Jesus is presented as the eternal word of God who became a human being and lived among us. In John's introduction Jesus is identified when it says, "In the beginning was the word, and the word was with God, and the word was God. The same was in the beginning with God. All things were made by him; and without him was not any thing made that was made. In him was life; and the life was the light of men." From the first chapter through the fourth chapter, Jesus was manifested to the world. In Chapters 5-12 He was manifested to the Jews. In Chapters 13-14 Jesus reveals himself fully to his disciples. The closing Chapters 18-21, tell of Jesus' arrest and trial, his crucifixion and resurrection, and his appearance to his disciples after the resurrection.

John emphasizes the gift of eternal life through Christ, a gift which begins now and comes to those who respond to Jesus. A striking feature of John is the symbolic use of common things from everyday life such as water, bread, light, the shepherd and his sheep, and the grapevine and its fruit to point to spiritual realities. In this scripture Jesus is the speaker. He is speaking to the Pharisees, a religious sect of Jews who were noted for their strict observance of the Mosaic law. In Chapter 9 Jesus had healed a man that was born blind. The miracle had been performed on the Sabbath Day. According to the Pharisees' interpretation Jesus had violated the Sabbath in several ways. First, Jesus made a paste out of clay and spittle; this was called work. Secondly, He had healed on the Sabbath; this was forbidden by the law except in emergencies.

After the miracle had taken place, the news spread like wild fire. When the Pharisees heard what had happened, they questioned the man. Not satisfied with the man's answers, they called in his parents. The parents said, "Ask him, he is of age," so they questioned him again. The man could only answer, "One thing I know, that whereas I was blind, now I see." Afterwards the Pharisees cast the man that had been blind out from the synagogue. When Jesus heard the news, He found the man and talked with him; as always just a little talk with Jesus makes it all alright. The Pharisees who were there heard the conversation. It was to these that Jesus was speaking when he told the parable of the good shepherd in Chapter 10. In this parable Jesus said, "I am come that they might have life and that they might have it more abundantly."

The scripture tonight is, "Jesus said unto him, I am the way, the truth, and the life: no man comes unto the Father, but by me" (John 14:6). I would like to concentrate on "Jesus: the way, the truth, and the life." The Biblical meaning of the word "way" is path or manner of life. To walk in the path that Jesus walked, we must go via the way of the cross. It was "At the cross, at the cross where I first saw the light, and the burdens of my heart rolled away. It was there, by faith, I received my sight, and now I am happy all the day." Going via the way of the cross is when we get our B. A. degree. I don't mean Bachelor of Arts; I mean "Born Again." After being born again and receiving the Holy Spirit as Jesus promised, we must go into the vineyard and work. Jesus said, "Behold I come quickly; and my reward is with me, to give every man according as his work shall be" (Revelation 22:12). To walk in the path that Jesus walked, we must deny ourselves, take up the cross, and follow him. If we walk in the way that Jesus walked, there are benefits. Psalm 19:7-9 says, "The law of the Lord is perfect, converting the soul: the testimony of the Lord is sure, making wise the simple. The statutes of the Lord are right, rejoicing the heart: the commandment of the Lord is pure, enlightening the eyes. The fear of the Lord is clean, enduring forever; the judgments of the Lord are true and righteous altogether."

Yes, God's way is the best way; God's way is the only way we can be saved. I am sure of this because, "The Lord is my shepherd; I have everything I need. He lets me rest in fields of green grass and leads me to quiet pools of fresh water. He gives me strength. He guides me in the right paths, as he has promised. Even if I go through the deepest darkness, I will not be afraid, Lord, for you are with me. Your shepherd's rod and staff protect me. You prepare a banquet for me, where all my enemies can see me; you welcome me as an honored guest and fill my cup to the brim. I know that your goodness and love will be with me all my life; and your house shall be my home as long as I live" (Psalm 23, *Good News Bible*).

Besides being the way, Jesus is also the truth. The Biblical meaning of the word "truth" is fact, real, or right. In stating a fact, we should, "Speak that we do know, and testify that we have seen" (John 3:11). We know that Jesus has saved us, and we do testify to that fact. Not only that but also when we pray and Jesus answers our prayers, we know that this is the real thing. On television they used to say that Coca Cola is the real thing; Jif tastes like peanuts; and margarine was better than butter. They even made cake mix moister and better than ever. The substitutes are so good that you can't tell them from the real thing. My friends, I want you to know that there is no substitute for Jesus. Jesus is the real thing; He is the best; I have tried him. He's at the top of my list, and I'd rather fight than switch. Yes, I know that Jesus is real; I know that He is truth. I also know that if we do as Jesus has instructed, everything will be right. In John 14:15-17 Jesus said, "If you love me, keep my commandments. And I will pray the Father, and he shall give you another comforter that he may abide with you forever. He is the Spirit, who reveals the truth about God. The world cannot receive him or know him. But you know him because he remains with you and is in you." John 8:32 says, "And you shall know the truth, and the truth shall make you free. "

Yes, Jesus is the way, the truth, and the life. The Biblical meaning of the word "life" is alive, living, a source, or cause or means of preservation. Some folks would rather have houses, land, motorcycles, and cars; some folks want silver and gold. Some folks think that life consists of an abundance of possessions. Yet, in spite of these things, some folks' lives are all messed up. Some folks are confused; some folks are frustrated, lonely, and possibly suicidal, looking for a fix, lovers of pleasure more than lovers of God, yet alive but without life. My friends, none of us is perfect; I know because I have been there, for "All have sinned and come short of the glory of God"

(Romans 3:23). Yet, in spite of our shortcomings there is a better life. To find the better life, don't consult Madam Bishop the palm reader or Dr. H. B. Woolscock the cure-all peddler who will sell you a remedy for anything and everything, but, rather, hear the word of the Lord, "I am come that you might have life and that you might have it more abundantly" (John 10:10b).

My friends, there is no life outside of God, for God is the Essence of life, the Giver of life, and the Sustainer of life. From God and God alone comes life. In order to truly appreciate life in all of its height, length, breadth, and depth, we should look at it like the psalmist in the 100the division. No one had to pressure him into thanksgiving; life is pressure enough in itself. So good was life that the psalmist would not be selfish in his praise, for he said, "Make a joyful noise unto the Lord, all lands." Life was so good to him that he wanted everyone everywhere to join him in celebrating. The psalmist knew that life is as high and lofty as God; it is as long as eternity; it is as broad as the universe; and it is as deep as the foundations of reality.

Life is also a serious and sacred matter. For that reason the poet said, "Know that the Lord he is God." One cannot take life lightly where there is a constant awareness "that the Lord he is God: it is he that has made us, and not we ourselves. We are his people and the sheep of his pasture" (vs. 3). Yes, God looks after and cares for us. Now we know that Jesus is the way, the truth, and the life, that we are his sheep who hear his voice and follow him, and that God in turn will give us eternal life. Jesus also wants us to know that it will not be an easy road. In this world you will have trials, tribulations, and sufferings. I Peter 3:17 says, "For it is better, if the will of God be so, that you suffer for well-doing, than for evil doing." Verse 4:19 continues, "Wherefore let them that suffer according to the will of God commit the keeping of their souls to him in well doing, as unto a faithful creator."

Yes, on this Christian journey life is like a mountain railroad with an engineer that's brave. We must make the run successful from the cradle to the grave. Watch the curves that fill the tunnel, never falter, never fail. Keep your hand upon the throttle and your eye upon the rail. Precious Savior, you will guide us 'til we reach the blissful shore where the angels wait to join us in your praise forevermore.

Yes, people, down through the ages there are those who can testify that Jesus is the way, the truth, and the life. Yes, Jesus is all of theses things and more, but to help you through the turns and curves, let me offer you some advice in a modified version of the poem **"If"**:

If you can trust when every one about you
Is doubting Him, proclaiming Him untrue;
If you can hope in Christ, tho' all forsake you,
And say 'tis not the thing for you to do;
If you can wait on God, nor wish to hurry,
Or, being greatly used, keep humble still;
Or if you're tested, still refuse to worry,
And so remain within His sovereign will

If you can say 'tis well when sorrow greets you,
And death has taken those you hold most dear;
If you can smile when adverse trials meet you,
And be content even tho' your lot be drear;
If you can be reviled and never murmur,
Or being tempted, nor give away to sin;

If you can fight for right and stand the firmer,
Or lose the battle when you ought to win,
And go to tell the story of the Savior
To souls in darkness over the desert dust;

If you can pray when Satan's darts are strongest,
And take the road of faith instead of sight;
Or walk with God, even tho' His way be longest,
And swerve neither to the left nor to the right;
If you desire Himself alone to fill you,
For Him alone you care to live and be;
Then 'tis not you, but Christ who dwelleth in you,
And that, O child of God, is victory! (Anonymous)

"Now the God of peace, that brought again from the dead our Lord Jesus, that great shepherd of the sheep, through the blood of the everlasting covenant, make you perfect in every good work to do his will, working in you that which is well pleasing in his sight, through Jesus Christ; to whom be glory forever and ever. Amen" (Hebrews 13:20-21).

IT TAKES PATIENCE TO HOLD ON AND HOLD OUT

Luke 21:19

Luke 21:19 - *In your patience possess your souls.*

The theme is taken from the third Gospel which puts emphasis upon the universality of Christ who embraces all humanity in his saving grace. It was written by Luke, a Greek whom Paul called "the beloved physician" (Colossians 4:14). Luke states his purpose early in the first chapter. *The English Version* reads: "Dear Theophilus: Many have done their best to write a report of the things that have taken place among us. They wrote what we have been told by those who saw these things from the beginning and proclaimed the message, and so Your Excellency, because I have studied all these matters from their beginning, I thought it good to write an orderly account for you. I do this so that you will know the full truth of all those matters which you have been taught."

Luke goes on to write about the conception of John the Baptist, his birth and naming, and his religious work. Luke also discusses the conception of Jesus, His baptism, temptation, and fasting. In Luke's report we also read about Jesus preaching, healing, calling of the twelve disciples, and many other things that Jesus both said and did. In our scripture tonight, which is found in the 21st chapter, Jesus is speaking about the widow who gave all that she had. He also foretells the destruction of the temple and about the troubles, persecutions, and tribulations that would come.

The 19th verse in *The King James Version* reads: "In your patience possess ye your souls." *The English Version* is "Hold firm, for this is how you will save yourselves." The chosen topic is "It Takes Patience to Hold On and Hold Out." In reading the Bible we find it to be an aid in Christian character building. II Timothy 3:16-17 says, "All scripture is given by inspiration of God, and is profitable for doctrine, for reproof, for correction, for instruction in righteousness: that the man of God may be perfect thoroughly furnished unto all good works." These words of the apostle Paul make it very clear that the Bible, besides being the history of redemption, is also our guide to the Christian's walk in life. Through this treasury of His wisdom, God guides us so that we may live as He would have us live. No matter what our situation in life, we have at hand, in the Bible, God's own word.

We also find that according to *The New Training for Service* there are certain divisions and classifications of the scripture. All scripture consists of:

1. Facts to be believed
2. Commands to be obeyed.
3. Promises to be received by those who believe the facts and obey the commands, and
4. Warnings to be heeded by all.

The scripture for tonight is number #3, a promise to be received by those who believe the facts and obey the commands. The promise is: "In your patience possess your souls or hold firm, for this is how you will save yourselves.

Questions that might be asked are: What is patience? Who gives us patience? What is the purpose of patience? We find that the word "patience" means constancy or endurance. It is also a synonym for longsuffering. In studying the word "patience" we found that it is a virtue; in fact, it is a difficult virtue to learn. Well, what do you mean by that? To have patience means waiting until God's time for everything, but we don't like to wait; we like speed. This is the day of instant products. We have instant coffee, instant tea, instant cake mix, instant potatoes, and many others. We want to see our life's hopes and dreams fulfilled on this instant basis.

Well, today, we would like to board a jet for a quick trip to Christian character. God permits pain and suffering to do their perfecting work, and that takes time. We would like to give our sons and daughters an education by writing out a check and letting them go to the university, have it cashed, and in return receive their diplomas, but laws of education say that the student must attend class and do homework; that takes time. We would like to see all men given a chance to voluntarily accept or reject Christ. God waits upon the willingness of his people, and that takes time. The song writer well-stated it when he said "You can't hurry God. Oh, no, you just have to wait. You have to trust Him and give Him time, no matter how long it takes. Now, He's a God you can't hurry. He'll be there; don't you worry. He may not come when you want Him, but He's right on time." "It takes patience to hold on and hold out."

My friends, who gives us patience? Patience is a gift, and it comes from God. Acts 2:38 tells us, "Repent and be baptized every one of you in the name of Jesus Christ for the remission of sins, and you shall receive the gift of the Holy Ghost." We know that the Holy Ghost is the Holy Spirit, and the Spirit has fruit. Galatians 5:22 says, "But the fruit of the Spirit is love, joy, peace, longsuffering" (which is patience). Fruit is a thing that produces or increases. Patience, being the fruit of the Spirit, is required for entrance into the Kingdom of God. II Peter 1:5-6 says, "And beside this, giving all diligence, add to your faith virtue, and to virtue knowledge; and to knowledge temperance; and to temperance patience." Friends, after finding that patience comes from God, we know that God is patient. In the book of Genesis we read of the creation of light and darkness, creation of the firmament, creation of the fruit of the earth, creation of the sun, moon, and stars, creation of fish and fowl, and creation of beasts and cattle. God made all of these things by the fifth day. On the sixth day He made man.

Notice, if you please, how patient God was in making man. With all of the other creations God said, "Let there be . . .," but with man He said, "Let us make man, in our own image, after our likeness." None of the other creations had this image and likeness; man was something special. Psalm 8:4-5 says, "What is man, that you are mindful of him? And the son of man that you visit him? For you have made him a little lower than the angels, and have crowned him with glory and honor." Not only did God crown man with glory and honor but I can see them, the God Head, the Trinity, in my mind's eye toiling over a lump of clay--molding and shaping it. I don't know what parts were made first, but I can see them working on each part, connecting the bones together. Then God Himself breathed into man's nostrils the breath of life. God took His time making man. God didn't hurry; He won't hurry unless He wants to hurry. The psalmist said in division 90:4, "For a thousand years in your sight are but as yesterday when it is past; and as a watch in the night." II Peter 3:8 says, "But beloved, be not ignorant of this one thing, that one day is with the Lord as a thousand years, and a thousand years as one day."

Not only was God patient but Jesus was also patient, and He is our example. I Peter 2:21 tells us, "For even hereunto were you called; because Christ also suffered for us, leaving us an example, that you should follow his steps." Jesus had patience with those who walked with him daily. There was Peter who denied him, contradicted Him, and even tried to correct Jesus, but the Lord loved Peter greatly, forgave him, and used him. Thomas doubted the resurrection, but the Lord did not reject him; instead, He appeared again when Thomas was present giving Thomas an opportunity to satisfy himself in that regard. Our Lord did definitely suffer, but rather than bring His suffering to an end by dealing with the offenders by wrath, He suffered long. He was patient and kind. "It takes patience to hold on and hold out."

Brothers and sisters, now that we know what patience means and who gives it, let us go on to the purpose of patience. Patience was not designed to make our pleasure less. Hebrews 10:36 tells us, "For you have need of patience, that after you have done the will of God, you might receive the promise." The purpose of patience is to help us to wait on God. Psalm 37:7 says, "Rest in the Lord, and wait patiently for him." Psalm 40:1 adds, "I waited patiently for the Lord; and he inclined unto me, and heard my cry." Lamentations 3:26 says, "It is good that a man should both hope and quietly wait for the salvation of the Lord."

The purpose of patience is not only for the layman but for the ministers also. II Corinthians 6:1-10 in *The English Version* is for the ministers. "In our work together with God, then, we beg of you: you have received God's grace, and you must not let it be wasted. Hear what God says: 'I heard you in the hour of my favor; I helped you in the day of salvation.' Listen! This is the hour to receive God's favor; today is the day to be saved. We do not want anyone to find fault with our work, so we try not to put obstacles in anyone's way. Instead, in everything we do we show that we are God's servants, by enduring troubles, hardships, and difficulties with great patience. We have been beaten, jailed, and mobbed; we have been overworked and have gone without sleep or food. By our purity, knowledge, patience, and kindness we have shown ourselves to be God's servants operating by the Holy Spirit, by our true love, by our message of truth, and by the power of God. We have righteousness as our weapon, both to attack and to defend ourselves. We are honored and disgraced; we are insulted and praised. We are treated as liars, yet we speak the truth; as unknown, yet we are known by all; as though we were dead, but, as you see, we live on. Although punished, we are not killed; although saddened, we are always glad; we seem poor, but we make many people rich; we seem to have nothing, yet we really possess everything." Ministers, it takes patience to hold on and hold out.

People, patience is just one avenue of the fruit of the Spirit which we need in order to travel on this Christian journey. Thank God, He is giving me patience to prepare in this world for the world to come. I'm reminded of a candy they make called "Now and Later". When you get tired of eating it now, you can put it up until later. Not so in the Christian life; Christian life is not a "now and later" situation. We must prepare and have patience to wait on God now. We do not know how long "now" is, but we do know that later is eternal. People, if you have patience, you cannot even begin to imagine the joys of eternal life on a perfect earth. Isaiah 65:17, 21, 23, 25 says, "For, behold, I create new heavens and a new earth: and the former shall not be remembered, nor come into mind. [. . .] And they shall build houses, and inhabit them; and they shall plant vineyards, and eat the fruit of them. [. . .]They shall not labor in vain, nor bring forth for trouble: for they are the seed of the blessed of the Lord, and their offspring with them. [. . .] The wolf and the lamb shall feed together, and the lion shall eat straw like the bullock: and dust shall be the serpent's meat. They shall not hurt nor destroy in all my holy mountain, said the Lord." Revelation 21:4 continues, "And God shall wipe away all tears from their eyes; and there shall be no more death, neither sorrow, nor crying, neither shall there be any more pain: for the former things are passed away." That's not all; I John 3:2 tell us, "Beloved, now are we the sons of God, and it does not yet appear what we shall be: but this we know, when Christ appears, we shall become like Him, because we shall see Him as He really is."

Finally, my sisters and my brothers, in order "to hold on and to hold out," I have found out that on this Christian journey the hills are hard to climb; enemies are all around us trying to get us down. I told the Lord that trouble is in my way, and you know, I have to cry sometimes, but through it all, I must tell Jesus. After telling Jesus, I learned how to lean and depend on him because He's a way maker. We find out all of these things on the way home. On the way home I might think that if I could just hold out 'til tomorrow, but I know I'm going to hold out because I'm standing on the promises of God. This old soul of mine is going home to live with my God. All of my troubles will be over. That's when I'll make a new start. People, "it takes patience to hold on and hold out."

Therefore, beloved, seeing you know these things before, beware lest you also, being led away with the error of the wicked, fall from your own steadfastness. But grow in grace, and in the knowledge of our Lord and Savior Jesus Christ. To him be glory both now and forever. Amen" (II Peter 17-18).

TIME UNKNOWN, BUT HAVE FAITH AND OBEY THE WORD OF THE LORD

Luke 19:13

Luke 19:13 - *And he called his ten servants, and delivered them ten pounds, and said unto them, Occupy till I come.*

In this scripture Jesus is speaking a parable. Jesus had often spoken of the Kingdom of God, and the people thought that the Kingdom of God would immediately appear. So, in Luke 19:12-13 He began a parable saying, "A certain nobleman went into a far country to receive for himself a kingdom and to return, and he called his ten servants, and delivered them ten pounds, and said unto them, Occupy till I come." The word "occupy" means to use or possess. The topic is "Time Unknown, But Have Faith and Obey the Word of the Lord."

This time conscious age wants to know the time or how long for everything. The questions of when was it or what time will it be are often heard. Man is rather adept at calculating time. A few years ago certain clocks were stopped long enough to give the earth time to catch up. Man knows what time comets will appear, when tides will rise and fall, and when the sun will rise and set. On an accurate scale he can plot the coming of fall, the migration of birds, and a host of other things. But, as to the coming of our Lord, the time is unknown. In Revelation 16:15 the scripture teaches us that He is coming as a thief--at an inconvenient and unannounced hour. If men knew the exact time of our Lord's return, many would be inclined to give a few minutes in service to Him; however, this service would be unacceptable because of improper motives. We worship God not out of fear of punishment but out of love and thanksgiving.

The only service pleasing to God is that given in response to His love, and great was that love. John 3:16 says, "For God so loved the world that He gave his only begotten son, that whosoever believes in him should not perish but have everlasting life." In response to God's love, man gives himself to God in worship and service. This is not done just for a few minutes but for a life time. So you see, the time of our Lord's return is unknown but sure. We have no urgent need to know neither the day nor the hour, but, while we are on this Christian journey, let Jesus guide, and let us make the best of what we have.

To make the best of what we have, we must first be born again. We must know God's will in our lives. The question was asked by Thomas, one of the disciples, of Jesus in John 14:5, "How can we know the way? Jesus answered; I am the way, the truth, and the life. No man comes unto the Father, but by me." The way to know God's will is to follow Him and obey His guidance. Psalms 37:5 say, "Commit your way unto the Lord; trust also in Him; and he shall bring it to pass." Proverbs 3:6 says, "In all your ways acknowledge him, and he shall direct your paths." Experience has taught me that prayer, the leadership of the Holy Spirit, the dedication of one's talent to the service of God, and entering open doors which God provides are ways to find the will of God. The will of God cannot be known by foresight like a railroad's tracks are seen before the engine's headlight. God's will is like the wake of a ship; the wake is the path or trail left behind in the water. Jesus has gone ahead and left a path to follow, and you must follow closely. The path is seen clearly only in our image which is manifested through the Holy Spirit; the voyage must be made by faith. It is the privilege of every child of God to have the guidance of the Holy Spirit at every turn of life. The conditions upon which that guidance is obtained is clearly stated or implied in James15:7, "If any of you lack wisdom, let him ask of God that gives to all men liberally, and upbraided not; and it shall be given him. But let him ask in faith, nothing wavering. For he that wavers is like a wave of the sea driven with the wind and tossed. For let not that man think that he shall receive anything of the Lord." The one who meets these conditions will be guided. Many of us make the mistake of wishing God to show us the whole way before we take the first step, but God leads a step at a time, and when we take the first step, He will make the next step clear.

Friends, have faith in God. These are more than mere words. They ring out this message loud and clear: If you keep faith in God, God will keep you. Hebrews 11:6 says, "But without faith it is impossible to please him; for he that comes to God must believe that he is, and that he is a rewarder of them that diligently seek him." We find that one is not born with an instinctive sense of trust. Trust is developed out of a situation where there is regularity, predictability, love, and fulfillment. If these conditions can be met time after time, one begins to develop certain expectancies, and continuous fulfillment of these experiences grows into a sense of trust. When that pattern of trust is fully established through experience, then that trust develops into faith. Out of a background of assured circumstances, one can then launch into the unknown with a feeling of assurance and confidence, with a feeling that says, "I know it will because I know *He* will."

When one thinks upon infancy, one can see something of the development of trust. As an infant looks forward to his feeding time, he begins to develop a pattern for eating. When whoever responds to his needs time after time with regularity, baby begins to know that person, and he develops confidence in her or him, whether mother, father, grandmother, or whoever. The child soon comes to know what to expect from that person. If mother is always there to satisfy his hunger, to make him comfortable, and to meet his emotional needs, baby's disposition begins to take shape and form a pattern of trust. He develops into a contented baby; he begins to know the person who makes him feel so contented. He begins to rely on this person; he begins to expect this person to meet his needs. His little mental machinery begins to develop the knowledge that "I know she or he will come--she always has -- she always will. Mind you, Baby does not respond to everyone around him; he will not allow some to even pick him up. However, he knows the one who provides for his comfort and well-being, and he counts on that person. He relaxes in the thought of his or her goodness, and he grows secure in the thought of that regularity. He can predict what tomorrow will bring; he has faith in her or his performance of duty--so he lies there cooing and smiling and facing the world with confidence.

The child of God might be likened unto this infant. When one experiences with regularity, time after time, the goodness of God, one becomes aware of the source of his blessings. He gets acquainted with God; he becomes knowledgeable of God's promises and aware of God's fulfillment. He learns about the experiences of others and how they have learned to trust. His own faith, therefore, begins to grow deeper and deeper. He goes forth with confidence feeling that he is strengthened by God's love and concern. He knows that in the fullness of time God will provide for all of his needs. With such good feelings one becomes aware of a relationship that exists between him and the source of goodness; one realizes, as does the infant, that one must respond to the relationship.

Just as Baby must open his mouth to receive the food, Christians must open their hearts to receive God's blessings. Just as the child learns to respond to the likes and wishes of his "comforter", the child of God seeks to know the will of his Father; he seeks to obey Him, to revere Him, and honor Him. He develops a sense of gratitude, and he continues to grow in knowledge, in stature, and in favor with God and man. Christian friends, an awareness of our own practice of faith in the daily grind of our everyday experiences will help one to grasp the meaning of faith. Our faith will enable us to see past what is and get a glimpse of what is to come. Faith enables us to see beyond the dismal now into the bright tomorrow. Faith is certain the ship is coming home to port although it cannot be seen at the moment. Faith lets us look through the storm into the balmy sunshine. Faith is like the motorist who approaches a bridge; he does not stop to examine or question its safety because others ahead of him crossed over without doubt, fear, or hesitation. He trusts the bridge because it has been tested by others. The same is true of the car you drive, the airplane you board, the chair you sit in; they have been tried and tested. Because they have been tried and tested, we can relax in the security of the silent promise of safety--so we trust; we believe; we venture.

To have faith in God is to rely upon and have unhesitating assurance of the truth of God's testimony even though it is unsupported by any other evidence and have unfaltering assurance of the fulfillment of His promises even though fulfillment seems impossible. The saints of old believed that God could cause the impossible to happen; do we? Paul admonished that under hopeless circumstances he hopefully believed. In these days of uncertainty, let us seek to increase our faith, to hold on, to endure, to believe that as God guides, He will provide. God has made a promise: "Him that comes unto me, I will in no wise cast out" (John 6:37). We are to keep on traveling for the master even when encountering detour signs along the way. We must not rely on our own wisdom to chart our course through life; rather, let the Holy Spirit be your guide. Romans 8:14 says, "For as many as are led by the spirit of God, they are the sons of God."

As earnest Christians we should be engaged in doing something for Christ even though we are surrounded by the frustrations of life. The Bible is filled with incidents of persons who had faith in God, obeyed Him, and made the best out of what they had. Matthew 3:3 tells us about John the Baptist; he used his voice, "The voice of one crying in the wilderness, prepare you the way of the Lord, make his paths straight." The twelve disciples of Jesus used what they had, God's word, to be fishers of men. Paul and Silas used what they had, which was prayer, to do missionary work and perform miracles for the Lord. John the Divine, on the Isle that was called Patmos, used what he had and made the most of his exile; he used his pen. Jesus Christ, our Lord and Savior, made the best of what He had in order to seek and save those that were lost; He gave His life as a ransom for many.

My friends let us, as children of God, "occupy" until Christ comes. Let us make the best out of what we have regardless of what it may be. Let us be sure that we are doing our very best, for then we will have the personal satisfaction of work well done. Each of us must bear some faults and burdens of our own; none of us is perfect. Don't be misled; remember that you can't ignore God and get away with it. A man will always reap just the kind of crop he sows. Let us not get tired of doing what is right, for after a while we will reap a harvest of blessings if we don't get discouraged and give up. Let us continue on this Christian journey doing our best to use or possess what the master has left us in charge of. As we do this, keep in mind the scripture in Ephesians 6:10-17: "Finally my brethren be strong in the Lord, and in the power of his might." We want to be strong to resist the enemy who will rob us of the good things that God gives to us. The scripture continues with, "Put on the whole armor of God that you may be able to stand against the wiles of the devil." It is this armor that gives us the ability to overcome Satan. My friends, Paul says, "We wrestle not against flesh and blood, but against principalities, against powers, against rulers of darkness of this world, against spiritual wickedness (wicked spirits) in high places."

Yes, we are to put on the whole armor that God has provided for the battle. The scripture describes the armor: "Put on the helmet of salvation; put on the breastplate of righteousness. Have your loins girt about with truth and your feet shod with the preparation of the gospel of peace, Take the sword of the Spirit, which is the word of God. Above all, take the shield of faith, wherewith you shall be able to quench all the fiery darts of the wicked one." Mark it down; the devil is on our trail. He is out to destroy our faith; that is why the Lord says, "above all, take the shield of faith. This equipment is absolutely essential to successful Christian living.

You may wonder how Satan can come upon you and overcome you when you are a child of God and the power of God is flowing through you. He cannot unless you have become weak. This is why Paul says, "Be strong in the Lord, and in the power of *his might*." The devil can't overcome you while you are strong. Here is the key; when he finds you weak, Satan will come and strip you of all your armor. Yes, you can be stripped of your armor since *you* were told *to put it on*. What is the armor that can prevent this? "Above all taking the shield of faith" is what we need. This is not downgrading any of the other pieces of armor. They are all important, but it is by the use of the shield of faith that we will be able to quench all the fiery darts of the enemy. This is the thing that the devil is out to take away from you first. The devil may never get you to drink, to rob a bank, or to run around with another person's spouse; he doesn't have to. If he can destroy your faith; he has you where he wants you.

This is what happened to Job; he let down his shield of faith a little bit. Satan fired on him in his conversation with his friends who were talking with him about his condition. In Chapter 23:2-4 Job said, "Even today is my complaint bitter: my stroke is heavier than my groaning. Oh that I knew where I might find him! That I might come even to his seat! I would order my cause before him, and fill my mouth with arguments." God listened to the conversation between these men, then God called Job in question in Chapter 38:3 and told him, "Gird up now your loins like a man; for I will demand of you, and you answer me. Where were you when I laid the foundations of the earth? Declare if you have understanding. Who laid the measures thereof, if you know? Or who has stretched the line upon it?" Job couldn't answer. God answered for Job in Chapter 40:1-2. "The Lord answered Job, and said, shall he that contended with the Almighty instruct him; he that reproves God let him answer it."

Friends, as we continue on this Christian journey, keep the words of this song in mind: "A charge to keep I have, A God to glorify, Who gave His Son my soul to save And fit it for the sky." Friends I can only tell you to do what the scripture tells us. "Put on the whole armor of God;" " Press toward the mark of a higher calling of God in Christ Jesus;" "Study to show yourself approved unto God, a workman that need not to be ashamed, rightly dividing the word of truth;" "Let brotherly love continue;" and above all, "Keep the faith."

Keep the faith because we are drawing from a deep well! Keep the faith because there might come a time God will say, "When you could, you wouldn't; now, you want to, but you can't!" Keep the faith; God has a penetrating eye! Keep the faith; we have to watch out for the snakes! Keep the faith because God was before it was a which, when, or where! Keep the faith; how can we escape if we neglect so great salvation! Keep the faith; we got to get right, stay right because the Lord just might come tonight, so don't let your feelings stand in the way of your faith! Keep the faith because there are three, the Father, the Son, and the Holy Spirit! Keep the faith; just keep toiling on and stepping out on faith because there's rest beyond the river! Keep the faith; nobody can do you like Jesus! Keep the faith if you know you've been born again! Keep the faith; the Lord saved you, and I know you're glad about it! Keep the faith; the Lord will help you to hold out!

Oh, yes, keep the faith my sisters and my brothers. Be constant in prayer that your faith will sustain you when your knowledge ceases to operate. Fight the good fight of faith; lay hold on eternal life. As for me, I, too, am going to keep the faith. I'm going through the school of true higher education on this Christian journey. I have a double minor of H.T.T. and C.B.--Hard Trials and Tribulation and Cross Bearing. I am going to get my major in E.L.--Eternal Life.

You see I stood by the wayside saying, "Pass me not, O gentle Savior, hear my humble cry; while on others thou are calling, do not pass me by." I'm going to work on until God says enough done, and when he calls me, I will answer. I'm going to cross over the chilly Jordan. I'm going to stop at the tree of life that bears twelve kinds of fruit and yield every month; the leaves of the tree are good for the healing of the nations. I'm going to move on up a little higher. I'm going to lay down my cross and get my crown. It will always be, "Howdy" and never, "Good-bye." *The time is unknown, but keep the faith, and obey the word of the Lord,* for He is Alpha and Omega, the beginning and the end, the first and the last. Amen.

THE POWER OF THE TONGUE:
WHAT IT'S ALL ABOUT

Luke 5:4-5

Luke 5:4-5 - *Now when he had left speaking, he said unto Simon, Launch out into the deep, and let down your nets for a draught, and Simon answering said unto him, Master, we have toiled all the night and have taken nothing; nevertheless at your word I will let down the net.*

The theme is "The Power of the Tongue; my subject is "What It's All About." We find in our theme scripture Jesus talking to one of the twelve that He chose name Simon (the Canaanite). We want to keep the names straight of the twelve because some of them had the same names. The names of all twelve can be found in Mark 3:16-19. We would also like to take note that they were chosen. There is a difference between being called and being chosen. Matthew 22:14 says, "For many are called but few are chosen."

So, we find Jesus speaking to one of the twelve whom he had chosen named Simon saying, "Launch out into the deep, and let down your nets for a draught." We are talking about the power of the tongue, and what it's all about. The word launch means to set a boat or ship afloat or to make a start. The starting or the beginning of all things was God. Genesis1:1, 3 say, "In the beginning God created the heaven and the earth, [. . .] and God said let there be," and it was. Then God made man and put him in a garden named Eden. Chapter 3:1-5 says, "Now the serpent was more subtle (shrewd, cunning) than any beast of the field which the Lord God had made. And he (the serpent) said unto the woman, yea has God said you shall not eat of every tree of the garden? And the woman said unto the serpent, we may eat of the fruit of the trees of the garden: But of the fruit of the tree which is in the midst of the garden God has said, you shall not eat of it, neither shall you touch it, lest you die. And the serpent said unto the woman, you shall not surely die: for God does know that in the day you eat thereof, then your eyes shall be opened, and you shall be as gods knowing good and evil"-- the power of the tongue.

The tongue is just as powerful now as it was then. We who are here tonight should be thankful to God that we have the privilege of speaking, hearing others speak, and understanding what they are saying. The faculty of speech certainly is one of the most precious gifts man can have. We shall see tonight that this faculty can be used for good or bad; it may be the source of blessings and also cursings. In different parts of the Bible, we have references to the use of the tongue. Proverbs 6:12-19 says, "A naughty person, a wicked man, walks with a forward mouth. He winks with his eyes, he speaks with his feet, he teaches with his fingers: Forwardness is in his heart, he devises mischief continually; he sows discord. Therefore shall his calamity come suddenly; suddenly shall he be broken without remedy. These six things doth the Lord hate: yea, seven are an abomination unto him: a proud look, a lying tongue, and hands that shed innocent blood, an heart that devises wicked imaginations, feet that be swift in running to mischief, a false witness that speaks lies, and he that sows discord among brethren'"--the power of the tongue.

Proverbs 15:1-7 says, "A soft answer turns away wrath: but grievous words stir up anger. The tongue of the wise uses knowledge aright: but the mouth of fools pours out foolishness. The eyes of the Lord are in every place, beholding the evil and the good. A wholesome tongue is a tree of life: but perverseness therein is a breach in the spirit. A fool despises his father's instruction; but he that regarded reproof is prudent. In the house of righteousness is much treasure: but in the revenues of the wicked is trouble. The lips of the wise disperse knowledge; but the heart of the foolish does not so."

James 3:1 says, "My brethren, be not many masters, knowing that you shall receive the greater condemnation. For in many things we offend all. If any man offend not in word, the same is a perfect man, and able also to bridle the whole body. Behold, we put bits in the horses' mouths that they may obey us; and we turn about their whole body. Behold also the ships, which though they be so great, and are driven of fierce winds, yet are they turned about with a very small helm, wherever the governor pleases. Even so the tongue is a little member and boasts great things. Behold how great a matter a little fire kindles! And the tongue is a fire, a world of iniquity: so is the tongue among our members, that it defiles the whole body, and sets on fire the course of nature: and it is set on fire of hell. For every kind of beasts, and of birds, and of serpents and of things in the sea, is tamed, and has been tamed of mankind: But the tongue can no man tame: it is an unruly evil, full of deadly poison," --the power of the tongue; no man, only God through the Holy Spirit can tame our tongue if we let Him--the power of the tongue.

My friends, I want to tell you tonight that the tongue is a powerful member of the body, a very small one, but it can be used for the glory and honor of God, Yes, God can tame the tongue. Knowing this, my friends, we should be steadfast in the faith. Hebrews 6:1 says, "Therefore leaving the principles of the doctrine of Christ, let us go on unto perfection: not laying again the foundation of repentance from dead works, and of faith toward God." It is time for us to leave the basics, to move forward, and grow in grace and knowledge. Allowing God to tame the tongue is a step toward Christian maturity. When you get to the point of no return, do as Moses did as he stood with the Egyptians at his back, the Red Sea in front of him, and the people grumbling. He didn't curse; he did as God told him to do. God told Moses to tell the people, "Fear not, stand still, and see the salvation of the Lord, which He will show to you today. For the Egyptians whom you have seen today, you shall see them no more forever. The Lord shall fight for you and you shall hold your peace."

Now, let me tell you what God did. He sent the Angel and the cloud that had been in front of them to the back of them, and it came between the Egyptians and the Israelites causing one not to see the other. Then Moses stretched out his hand over the sea, and God called the east wind. Let me pause and tell you about these winds. There are four winds: the north winds, the south wind, the west wind, and the east wind. Each serves a purpose. The cold north winds dispersed rain clouds. The south wind was regarded as the sign of hot weather. The cool west wind brought rain. The east wind was hot and sultry; coming over the Arabian Desert, it affected vines and vegetation. This is the wind that God called. The east wind blew all that night and made a wall out of the water and a highway upon the dry ground--the power of the tongue.

Now, people, let us look at three men who knew the power of the tongue and what it was all about. The book of Daniel, the third chapter, tells about Shadrach, Meshach, and Abednego. King Nebuchadnezzar asked them if it was true that they did not serve his gods, nor worship the golden images which he had set up. The decree was restated as the story continues in verse 15b, "Now when you hear the sound of the music, you fall down and worship the image which I have made; but if you worship not, you shall be cast into the midst of a burning fiery furnace; and who is that God that shall deliver you out of my hands? Shadrach, Meshach, and Abednego answered and said to the king, I want you to hear me now O Nebuchadnezzar, we are not careful to answer you in this matter. If be so our God whom we serve is able to deliver us from the burning fiery furnace, and he will deliver us out of your hand, O King. But if not, be it known unto you, O king, that we will not serve your gods, nor worship the golden image which you have set up"- -the power of the tongue.

My brothers and my sisters, this is what it's all about. You have seen and heard advertisements about pleasing the physical body. They even tell you that for people you need look in the yellow pages. But you can't find this in the yellow pages: the recipe for the Bread of Life. This recipe has no food value like vitamin A, B, or C, but it is the most important part of your diet. It is good for your vision, your hearing, and your senses of smelling, feeling, and taste. In John 9:25, "The blind man said one thing I know, whereas I was blind, now I see." Psalms 4:3 says, "The Lord will hear when I call unto him." Philippians 4:18 tells us, "But I have all, and abound: I am full, having received of Epaphroditus the things which were sent from you, an odor of a sweet smell, a sacrifice acceptable, well pleasing to God." Luke 24:32 says, "And they said one to another, did not our heart burn within us, while he talked with us by the way, and while he opened to us the Scriptures." Psalms 34:8 invites us to, "O taste and see that the Lord is good."

My friends, some of you might be like me and this song: "a long, long time ago, my heart was troubled with sin. My head was bowed down in sorrow; the devil had me wrapped up in sin. I started out to seek salvation; I had a hard time resisting temptation, but kept on searching 'til I found the King of Kings." My pastor always tells the story of how he got saved when he was a little boy in the state of Mississippi. Well, I was a little bitty girl down in the state of Mississippi. I won't tell the whole story but just enough to let you see the power of the tongue. Each year we had a three weeks revival, and I had been sitting on what was called the "mercy seat" for three years. I wanted to have a great conversion, one that everybody was going to be talking about, but it didn't happen that way. Some had come through seeing stars shining in the day time; some the Lord had woke up at a certain time, and others a dark cloud came over the sun. Some even crossed hell on a spider web; you've heard those testimonies. Nothing like that happened to me. I was told to stop playing and find myself a praying ground. My mother warned me that if I was not saved, I couldn't go to heaven. She even told me a story about her brother who she believed died and went to hell because he died shooting dice. That was scary, but that didn't do it for me. I'm still talking about the power of the tongue. Finally, in the third year going into the third week, the last week of this revival, an old deacon spoke to us; I remember so well. It was that Tuesday night when the old deacon told us, "Children, you all don't have any great big sins, and you haven't committed any crimes. All you have to do is believe in your heart that the Lord will save you, and I declare He will." At that moment I stood up on faith; I didn't have but just a little bit, but I stood up and launched out. You know, I can only try to imagine within my mind how Jesus must have felt as he hung on the cross for you and me with the weight of the sins of the world on His shoulders. They nailed His feet; they speared Him in His side, but oh, when they got to His hands and nailed them, He looked to His Father and said, "It is finished." God lifted the weight of sin off His shoulders. That's the way that God did me. When I stood up, I tell you, I hadn't seen anything, but I felt the change, that sense of feeling a weight lifted off my shoulders. You talking about being on cloud nine; the Lord saved me, and I'm glad about it--the power of the tongue, and what it's all about, the power of God. God told Moses to speak to the rock; Jesus told us to speak to the mountain--the power of the tongue, and what it's all about, the power of God.

Before I close, I want you to know that John the Divine, John the Revelator, or "I" John as my daddy used to say or whichever one you want to call him said in Revelation 1:8-11, "I am Alpha and Omega, the beginning and the ending said the Lord, which is, which was, and which is to come, the Almighty. I, John, who also am your brother and companion in tribulation, and in the Kingdom and patience of Jesus Christ, was in the isle that is called Patmos, for the word of God, and for the testimony of Jesus Christ. I was in the Spirit on the Lord's day, and heard behind me a great voice as of a trumpet, Saying, I am Alpha and Omega, the first and the last: What you see, write in a book, and send it to the seven churches which are in Asia; [. . .]" This brings us back to the recipe for the Bread of Life that definitely attests to effecting vision and hearing and demonstrates the power of the tongue.

Jesus declared in John 5:35, "I am the Bread of Life: he that comes to me shall never hunger: and he that believes on me shall never thirst." The ingredients in this bread are 100% pure. It has no artificial preservatives or refined sugar. It is guaranteed through all times. Eat it all; be sure that none is thrown away or end up in the garbage disposal. The ingredients are: repentance, belief, and baptism. Wrap it in the Holy Ghost and put it in Jesus. As you partake of this bread, you will find that it is the roughage or the bulk in your diet whether you are milk fed or meat fed. It is the outer coating and inner core of your being. To this diet add patience, experience, hope, and love; eat it, and digest the whole loaf. As you eat, be sure you are fully clothed having girt your loins with truth, put on the breast plate of righteousness, and having the gospel of peace on your feet. Take the shield of faith, the helmet of salvation, and the sword of the Spirit, which is the word of God; people, this is what it's all about.

"Now unto him that is able to do exceeding abundantly above all that we ask or think, according to the power that works in us, unto him be glory in the church by Jesus Christ throughout all ages, world without end. Amen" (Ephesians 3:20-21).

TO WHOM ARE YOU LOOKING, AND WHAT ARE YOU LOOKING FOR? - Perspective I

Isaiah 45:22

Isaiah 45:22 - *Look unto me, and be saved, all the ends of the earth: for I am God, and there is none else.*

Man was originally endowed with noble powers and a well-balanced mind. He was perfect in his being and in harmony with God. His thoughts were pure, his aims holy. But, through disobedience his powers were perverted and selfishness took the place of love. So, Man finally came to the realization that he was in the pit of sin, and it was impossible to escape. God intervened and sent His Son to redeem man from this sinful state. Jesus extended an invitation saying, "Look unto me, and be saved, all the ends of the earth: for I am God and there is none else" (Isaiah 45:22). Upon many ears there fall the words of the gracious invitation, "Look unto me"-- that call of a compassionate Savior whose heart of love is drawn out toward all who are standing at the crossroads and wondering which way to go.

In the hearts of many who are really longing for the help to be found in Jesus, there is quickened the purpose to return to the Father's house. With such people the inquiry of Thomas is often repeated, "How can we know the way?" The Father's house seems to be a long way off and the road appears difficult and uncertain. What are the steps which lead homeward?

Let us not despair neither let us say as Israel said in Ezekiel 37:11, "Our bones are dried, and our hope is lost; we are cut off for our parts." Rather, say the same as Paul said in Romans 10:1, "Brethren my hearts desire and prayer to God for [us] is, that [we] might be saved." In our discussion of the steps which lead homeward, we will look at the steps that have been taken, and then we will look at the steps to take.

In the beginning God spoke directly to man. "God also has spoken at different times , and in different manners in times past by the prophets, but in these last days has spoken to us by His Son, whom he has appointed heir of all things" (Hebrews 1:1-2). The message says, "Look unto me, and be saved." How can we be saved? The only way that we can be saved is the way that Jesus said in John 3:5, "Except a man be born of water and of the Spirit, he cannot enter into the Kingdom of God." Acts 2:38 calls for us to "Repent and be baptized every one of you in the name of Jesus Christ for the remission of sins, and you shall receive the gift of the Holy Ghost." Romans 10:9-10 explains further "That if you shall confess with your mouth, and shall believe in your heart that God has raised him from the dead you shall be saved. For with the heart man believes unto righteousness and with the mouth confession is made unto salvation." "Look unto me and be saved" not only applies to us today but to all generations--past, present, and future. Romans 10:8 says, "The word is near you, even in your mouth, and in your heart: that is the word of faith which we preach. If we are to be saved, we must have faith." Hebrews 11:6 tells us, "But without faith it is impossible to please him: for he that comes to God must believe that he is and that he is a rewarder of them that diligently seek him."

In order to be saved there are some guidelines that we are to go by. Isaiah 55:6 says, "Seek the Lord while he may be found, call upon him while he is near. Samuel said in I Samuel 12:24, "Only fear the Lord, and serve him in truth with all your heart." Mark 5:36 adds, "Jesus said be not afraid only believe." Luke 5:4 tells us, "Jesus said, Launch out into the deep and let down your nets." Paul said in Acts 27:31, "Except these abide in the ship, you cannot be saved." We can do these things no matter what the weather may be, rain or shine, snow or sleet because Ecclesiastes 11:4 says, "He that observes the wind shall not sow: and he that regards the clouds shall not reap." We do not stop when we become saved; we just keep moving on up higher.

As we move on, let us keep these things in mind: to move up you must have a mind to work and must be willing to learn. Isaiah 28:10 explains, "For precept must be upon precept, line upon line, here a little and there a little, trust not in false security." Verse 20 goes on with, "For the bed is shorter than that a man can stretch himself in it: and the covering narrower than that he can wrap himself in it." But, rather let us listen and learn. As we walk we can hear a word behind us in Isaiah 30:21 urging us, "This is the way, walk in it, when you turn to the right hand, and when you turn to the left." As we move up we can say as David said in Psalm 5:7, "My heart is fixed, O God my heart is fixed: I will sing and give praise." Keep praising Him as you move up because, you see, if you don't praise Him, the rocks will cry out.

As we move up let us just keep so busy working for the Savior. As we move up, if we get tired, Isaiah 40:31 assures us that "They that wait upon the Lord shall renew their strength; they shall mount up with wings as eagles; they shall run and not be weary; and they shall walk; and not faint." "Look unto me and be saved for I am God, and there is none else." In keeping with our theme, "To Whom Are You Looking, and What Are You Looking For," friends, I am looking to Jesus, the author and finisher of our faith. The reason I am looking to Him is because He said in Isaiah 61:1-3, "The Spirit of the Lord God is upon me; because the Lord has anointed me to preach good tidings unto the meek; he has sent me to bind up the brokenhearted, to proclaim liberty to the captives, and the opening of the prison to them that are bound; To proclaim the acceptable year of the Lord, and the day of vengeance of our God; to comfort all that mourn; To appoint unto them that mourn in Zion, to give unto them beauty for ashes, the oil of joy for mourning, the garment of praise for the spirit of heaviness; that they might be called trees of righteousness, the planting of the Lord, that he might be glorified."

My friends, if that isn't enough, just think about what Jesus suffered for our sake. In verse 53:1-3 Isaiah asks, "Who has believed our report? And to whom is the arm of the Lord revealed? For he shall grow up before him as a tender plant, and as a root out of a dry ground: he hath no form nor comeliness: and when we shall see him, there is no beauty that we should desire him. He is despised and rejected of men, a man of sorrows, and acquainted with grief: and we hid as it were our faces from him, and we esteemed him not." Yet in spite of all of this John 1:1, 4, 10-12 says, "In the beginning was the word and the word was with God, and the word was God. [. . .] In him was life: and the life was the light of men. [. . .] He was in the world and the world was made by him, and the world knew him not. He came unto his own, and his own received him not. But as many as received him, to them gave he power to become the sons of God, even to them that believe on his name." Jesus came to John to be baptized in the river of Jordan. I can see John when Jesus stepped in the water. When John raised his hands he might have said like some do, "Obedience to the great head of the church; I baptize you, my brother . . ." After the baptism Jesus went about preaching repentance for the remission of sins, healing all manner of diseases, making the lame to walk, and the dumb to talk. "Look unto me and be saved for I am God, and there is none else."

You know, somewhere or sometimes along the way you may have struggles, but looking to Jesus, guess what? "We are troubled on every side, yet not distressed, we are perplexed, but not in despair, persecuted, but not forsaken, cast down, but not destroyed," (II Corinthians 4:8-9). Knowing this, every once in a while just look up. "Look up and be saved for I am God, and there is none else." Jesus Himself knew troubles, and He is our example. It looked bad for a while, but what a glorious ending! As Jesus went about doing only good, some people began to get jealous so they plotted how they would kill him. After having gone from court to court and from judgment hall to judgment hall, this great God, the same whose Spirit moved upon the face of the waters and said, "Let there be light, and there was light," who divided the waters from the waters, this Great God died for you and me. Jesus enabled us to come boldly before Him after the day's work is done, and it's time to unwind. He will quietly and calmly say to us, "Be still and know that I am God" (Psalm 46:10). "In quietness and confidence we shall be strengthened" (Isaiah 30:15). "The eternal God is your refuge, and underneath are the everlasting arms" (Deuteronomy 33:27a). "Peace I leave with you, my peace I give unto you: not as the world gives, give I unto you. Let not your heart be troubled, neither let it be afraid" (John 14:27). "The peace of God, which surpasses all understanding shall keep your hearts and mind through Christ Jesus" (Philippians 4:7). "Look unto me and be saved [. . .]."

My brothers and my sisters, I would like for you to know that I am still looking to God for everything that I need. I would like for you to know that God is good to me. I would like for you to know that God has answered some of my prayers; that's the reason I like the 5th Sunday. Every time a fifth Sunday rolls around at my church that's when all choirs sing. When they have the processional, I look, and when I look, I can see three generations marching up before God. When I look, I say just like Adam said when he looked at the woman that God gave him: "That's bone of my bones and flesh of my flesh because many of them are my children and grandchildren who God has allowed me to live to see. I would like for you to know today that "I have never reached perfection, but I've tried;/ sometimes I have lost connection, but I've tried. / Sometimes right and sometimes wrong, hoping someday to be strong./ Then, I'll rise and sing this song: Lord, I've tried." Saints, let us pray this prayer as we go through: "Let the words of my mouth and the meditation of my heart be acceptable in your sight." " Now the God of peace, that brought again from the dead our Lord Jesus, that great shepherd of the sheep, through the blood of the everlasting covenant, make you perfect in every good work to do his will, working in you that which is well-pleasing in his sight, through Jesus Christ to whom be glory for ever and ever. Amen" (Hebrews 13:20-21).

TO WHOM ARE YOU LOOKING, AND WHAT ARE YOU LOOKING FOR? - Perspective II by E. Y. James

Isaiah 45:22

Isaiah 45:22 - *Look unto me, and be saved, all the ends of the earth: for I am God, and there is none else.*

My friends, the first question is, "To whom are you looking?" The question implies that there must be more than one choice. Let's begin by looking at Matthew 6:24 which say, "No man can serve two masters for either he will hate the one, and love the other, or else he will hold to one, and despise the other. You cannot serve God and mammon"(material things). So, with these two choices in mind, the question remains, "To whom are you looking?" Many people in the world today are looking for something better. They are not satisfied with the world and the shape it's in and are not satisfied with themselves and the shape they are in. This includes rich, wealthy, well-to-do, middle class, lower class, and poverty-stricken peoples all over the world. They are not satisfied, and they do not know where to turn or to whom to turn. The devil has them wrapped up, tied up, tangled up, and shackled up in their minds, and they are thinking that there is no help.

Some have turned to the President, but all of the presidents in the world have failed in some way to completely do the job assigned to them. There is no failure in God. Man cannot end the wars or poverty or any of the critical problems of the world; they can find no permanent solutions. Many people, especially our young people, have turned to alcohol, drugs, marijuana, and many other forms of escapes from reality. To whom have you turned or what? People cannot cope with the situation so they "cop out" and become drop outs from schools and society at large. Satan has convinced these people that there is no other answer. I say to you, "For the Lord God omnipotent reigneth." To **whom** are **you** looking? "No man can serve two masters. [. . .] You cannot serve God and mammon." To **whom** are **you** looking?

People have confused minds because Satan has convinced them that they can have their cake and eat it, too, but he never tells them how they can do the impossible. People, we want the world and all of its (what the devil calls) good things without including the bad things. We don't know how to get what we want out of life. Many times when we don't know how to get what we want out of life, we try to escape from the reality that all things are in the world, and we can only survive through God. Christians are supposed to be *in* the world but not *of* the world. But Satan says that you can be both. To whom are you looking? You cannot serve two masters just as you cannot go to both heaven and hell. The choice is yours! To whom are you looking?

Our theme scripture states, "Look unto me, and be saved, all the ends of the earth; for I am God, and there is none else. Look unto me, for I am God." Today, yes, right now, we should look unto God. The solution to all of our problems lies in God's hands. People look to every thing and every person **before** they look to God. Those who have turned to drugs, alcohol, marijuana, horoscopes, and others, I say to you to look to God! God has all power in His hands. God can do what no man can do. Matthew 6:27 asks, "Which of you, by taking **thought** can add one cubit unto his stature?" Can man just think and make himself grow an inch or two? Verse 5:36 says, "Neither shall you swear by the head, because you can not make one hair white or black." God can do what no man can do. Ecclesiastes 7:13 tells us to "Consider the work of God; for who can make that straight which he has made crooked?" We cannot keep the trees from turning green in the spring nor can we keep them from shedding their leaves or being as if they are dead in the winter. All that man knows and has done, he has not been able to significantly change in any way the natural forces of nature. He can't make the wind blow or stop it. John 3:8 says, "The wind blows where it pleases, and you hear the sound thereof, but can not tell whence it comes and where it goes."

To Christians and non-Christians, to all, especially you young people, look to God. If you feel that you must do a little lying and a little cheating to "get by", remember what Romans 12:1-2 says, "I Beseech you therefore my brethren by the mercies of God, that you present your bodies a living sacrifice, holy, acceptable unto God, which is your reasonable service." We just can't do any and everything and call ourselves the servants of God. "And be not conformed to this world; but be transformed by the renewing of your mind, that you may prove what is that good and acceptable and perfect, will of God." We do not have to conform to the sins of the world to meet our needs.

If you would only look to God, He will take care of your every need and desire. Matthew 6:20 says, "Wherefore, if God so clothe the grass of the field, which today is, and tomorrow is cast into the oven, shall he not much more clothe you, O you of little faith." To whom are you looking? Verse 25 adds, "Therefore I say unto you, take no thought for your life, what you shall eat, or what you shall drink; nor yet for your body, what you shall put on. Is not the life more than meat, and the body than raiment? Behold the fowls of the air, for they sow not, neither do they reap, nor gather into barns; yet your heavenly Father feeds them. Are you not better than they?" If this is true, then to whom are you looking? Look to God for all. Verse 28 asks, "And why take you thought for raiment? Consider the lilies of the field, how they grow; they toil not, neither do they spin, and yet I say unto you, that even Solomon in all his glory was not arrayed like one of these." Who can look more beautiful than a flower? To *whom* are you looking? Look to God for everything. I admonish you as in verse 31, "Therefore take no thought, saying, what shall we eat? Or what shall we drink? Or wherewithal shall we be clothed? For after these things do the Gentiles seek, for your heavenly Father knows that you have need of all these things." Need I say more? Have you got the picture?

Personally, I am looking to God, a God with everything in His hands. David said in Psalm 24, "The earth is the Lord's and the fullness thereof, the world, and they that dwell therein." God has everything. All we have to do is keep his commandments and live the kind of life so that we can get what we want. Matthew 7:7 says, "Ask and it shall be given." If this is God's promise, and hopefully by now you have decided to look to God because he is fully able to take care of your needs, then the question remains, what are you looking for? Isaiah 45:22 says, "Look unto me and be saved, all the ends of the earth: for I am God, and there is none else." Look unto me, and

be saved! Are you saved? If you are, fine; if not, are you looking to be saved? If you are not saved, then, what are you waiting on; what are you looking for? Matthew 6:33 tells us, "But seek first the Kingdom of God and his righteousness; and all these things shall be added to you. None of God's promises except wrath is to the unsaved so get saved; salvation is what you should be looking for. To those who are saved, what are *you* looking for? Seek first the Kingdom of God and His righteousness, and God will take care of the rest. If we would only put God first, we would get everything that we need. So, what we should be looking for is "the Kingdom of God and His righteousness."

I don't know what you are looking for, but I am like Paul in Philippians 3:13-14, "Brethren, I count not myself to have apprehended: but this one thing I do, forgetting those things which are behind (the sins of the worldly life) and reaching forth unto these things which are before. I press toward the mark for the prize of the high calling of God in Christ Jesus." I want to change the question and personalize it; what am **I** looking for? I can tell you what I am looking for. I am looking for God to do as David requested in Psalm 51:10, "Create in me a clean heart O, God and renew a right spirit in me." What am I looking for? I am looking for "The Road Not Taken" as the poet Robert Frost writes in his poem:

Two roads diverged in a yellow wood and sorry I could not travel both (no man can serve two masters)
And be one traveler. Long I stood and looked down one as far as I could
To where it bent in the undergrowth, (Both look pretty good when you are starting out; sometimes Satan's road looks even better.)
But took the other as just as fair, and having perhaps the better claim
Because it was grassy and wanted wear ("few there be that find it").
Two roads diverged in a wood and I - I took the one less traveled by
And that has made all the difference.

I am looking for the entrance to this road. What am I looking for? I am looking for the gate called strait. In Matthew 7:13-14 Christ said, "Enter in at the strait gate; for wide is the gate and broad is the way that leads to destruction, and many there be which go in thereat; Because strait is the gate and narrow is the way, which leads to life, and few there be that find it." The only way you can find the entrance to life is that you must be born again. If you believe that Jesus died on the cross, shed his blood, and rose again for you, you have been born of the blood. I have truly washed my soul in the blood of the Lamb of God. I was born of the water when I was

12 years old. When the Holy Ghost, called the Comforter, entered my life, I was born of the Spirit. When all of this happened, the Comforter led me to the entrance to life, and now I am traveling the "The Road Not Taken", the narrow way, or that highway. While I am on this road, I want to be a bold soldier for Christ, so if God asks as He did in Isaiah 6:9-8, "I heard the voice of the Lord saying whom shall I send, and who will go for us?" I want to answer as the writer, "Then said, I, Here am I; send me and he said Go." I am willing to run all the way.

I want you to know that if you would but look to God, He can save you. Isaiah 59:1-2 says, "Behold the Lord's hand is not shortened that it cannot save; neither his ear heavy that it cannot hear: But your iniquities have separated between you and your God, and your sins have hid his face from you, that he will not hear." If you are unsaved, just give up, give in, and look to God; He will hear your cry. If you are saved, but you can't seem to get a prayer through, and if there seems to be no answer to any of your needs or desires, check out your life and your sins. When you are weighed in the balance, will you be found wanting? Look to God; He can clean you up if you would only let Him. God is not going to enter by force but only if you are willing to let Him work in your life. Revelation 3:20 says, "Behold, I stand at the door, and knock: if any man hear my voice, and open the door, I will come in to him, and will sup with him, and he with me." You must be willing; you must open the door. You should be looking for a Savior today. "To day, if you will hear his voice, harden not your hearts" (Hebrews 4:7b).

Friends, I have found the Savior, so what else am I looking for? I am looking for a life in Christ Jesus that is so true and so real that I can pray like Hezekiah did when the Lord told him it was his time to die. Isaiah 38:3 records what Hezekiah said; "Remember now, O Lord, I beseech you, how I have walked before you in truth and with a perfect heart and have done that which is good in your sight." Oh, Saints, how is your walk? I want to get an answer like Hezekiah did in verse 5, "Thus said the Lord, I have heard your prayer, I have seen your tears; behold I will add unto your days 15 years." God knows what we are going through. He sees our tears, and he knows the deep secrets of our hearts. I don't want to leave with my work undone; I want to finish every task and answer every call that God has given me. I may have something that I desire to do or finish before I leave. What about my children or even grandchildren; are they saved? I may be needed to show them the way. I may be old and gray, but I may still be a light to someone that needs a light or counseling right then. Lord, just let me see this thing through, and then I'll be ready.

What are you looking for? This I do not know, but I am also looking for the wisdom, knowledge and understanding that comes from God. I want to open my mouth and let God speak through me; I want the Lord to use me. Saints, I am looking for that day, early in the morning when I rise, I'll shake the dust from my feet, be caught up in a cloud as I'm riding on my two wings. I will have exchanged mortal for immortality and checked my flesh into the Lost and Found; you know, I once was lost, but now I'm found. I want to stop and get fitted for my new clothes, you know, when I can take off my breastplate of righteousness, lay down my shield of faith, put aside the sword of the spirit, and trade all these in for a long white robe. Then I want to take off those shoes that were prepared with the gospel of peace and exchange them for my golden slippers. I'll take off my helmet of salvation and trade it in for my golden crown or crowns because there are more than one. Then, I will make my way to the throne of God where I can make the soul check. Just like we used to check our coats at certain events, I am going to check my tears; I won't have to cry any more. I'm going to check my hurt, hunger, and pain, for Revelation 7:16 says, "They shall hunger no more, neither thirst any more; neither shall the sun light on them nor any heat for the Lamb which is in the midst of the throne shall feed them and shall lead them unto living fountains of waters: and God shall wipe away all tears from their eyes." As I am walking around and I pass by what Paul says in II Corinthians 5:1,"[. . .] that building of God, a house not made with hands, eternal in heaven;" you know, I am talking about my mansion, an angel might ask me, "What are you looking for?" I can say that I am looking for the one Solomon called the Rose of Sharon and the Lily of the Valley (Song of Solomon 2:1); I am looking for the one Isaiah said, "[. . .] and his name shall be called Wonderful, Counselor, The Mighty God, The Everlasting Father, The Prince of Peace" (9:6b). I am looking for the one that John said, "[. . .] and his name shall be called The Word of God and on his thigh a name written King of Kings and Lord of Lords" (Revelation 19:13b, 16). I am looking for the one better known to me as Jesus because He's the one who died for me. What are **you** looking for?

I AM; YOU ARE; ABIDE IN ME

John 15:1-2

John 15:1-2 - *I am the true vine and my Father is the husbandman. Every branch in me that bears not fruit he takes away: and every branch that bears fruit he purges it, that it may bring forth more fruit,*

In the first book of Moses called Genesis, we read in Chapter1:1, "In the beginning God created the heaven and the earth." Further down we find that on the sixth day He made man in His own image and after His own likeness, blessed man and gave him dominion over the world. Everything was perfect until the deceiver came along. After having been deceived by the devil, after the shameful fall from the status that God had placed man, and after this loss of paradise, God promised man a redeemer. This redeemer was born forty-two (42) generations from the time of Abraham. His name was Jesus, a name selected by God. After His birth Jesus grew not only in stature but also in knowledge and in favor with God and man. At the age of twelve, He began to be about His Father's business. At the age of thirty, He came preaching repentance and baptism with water, with the Holy Ghost, and with fire. He came teaching us that man shall not live by bread alone but by every word that proceeded out of the mouth of God. He came teaching us to pray, "Our Father which art in heaven." He came teaching us to beware of false prophets which come to you in sheep's clothing. He came teaching that heaven and earth shall pass away but God's word shall stand forever. He came teaching us that God is love. With all of these things that Jesus came preaching and teaching, He is saying to us: "I am; you are; abide in me."

I would like for you to know tonight that we are not the only ones who have come in contact with this "I am." If Moses were here, He could tell you that one day as he was leading his father-in-law's flock to the backside of the desert, he came to the mountain of God, "And the angel of the Lord appeared unto him in a flame of fire out of the midst of a bush: and he looked, and the bush burned with fire and the bush was not consumed. And Moses said I will now turn aside, and see this great sight, why the bush is not burnt" (Exodus 3:2-3). I imagine Moses had seen fires before on his daily occupation. It is hot in this country, and there is such a thing as spontaneous combustion, but he had never seen anything like this. When he turned aside to see, "God called unto him out of the midst of the bush, and said, Moses, Moses. And he said here am I. And he said, Draw not near here: put off your shoes from off your feet, for the place whereon you stand is holy ground. Moreover he said, I am the God of your father, the God of Abraham, the God of Isaac, and the God of Jacob" (vs. 4b-6a). God continued to talk to Moses and told Moses what he wanted him to do. Then Moses began to talk to God. At first Moses was afraid to look upon the face of God, but after God told him to go back to Egypt, he was more afraid of the man he was to face than he was of God. So in verses 11, 13-14 Moses asked God, "Who am I, that I should go [. . .], and when I start telling them the God of your fathers sent me, and they ask me what is his name? what shall I say unto them? And God said unto Moses, I AM THAT I AM, tell them I AM sent me." I am; you are; abide in me.

We could continue to speak of all of the old men of renown, but let us continue with our theme scripture, John 15:2, "I am the true vine and my Father is the husbandman. Every branch in me that bears not fruit he takes away and every branch that bears fruit he purges it, that it may bring forth more fruit." The writings of this book are attributed to John, the disciple whom Jesus loved. Let us note, if you please, that John began his writings with, "In the beginning was the word, and the word was with God, and the word was God." As John continued to write, he did not write in the same fashion as the other three gospel writers: Matthew, Mark, and Luke. John's writings had a deeper explanation of what Jesus said and did.

The setting is the upper room where Jesus had met with his disciples on the Passover eve. Jesus began to talk to his disciples for he knew that his hour had come when he would soon be taking his departure back to

His Father. As he talked he wrapped a towel around himself and began to wash his disciples' feet. He sent away the traitor and began to prepare the eleven for His coming death and resurrection. In Chapter 14:1-9, Jesus told his disciples, "Let not your heart be troubled: you believe in God, believe also in me. In my Father's house are many mansions: if it were not so, I would have told you. I go to prepare a place for you, and if I go and prepare a place for you, I will come again, and receive you unto myself: that where I am there you may be also, and where I go you know, and the way you know. Then Thomas said unto him, Lord we know not where you go, and how can we know the way? Jesus said unto him, I am the way, the truth, and the life: no man comes unto the Father, but by me, If you had known me, you should have known my Father also. Phillip said unto him, Lord show us the Father, Jesus said unto him Have I been so long time with you, and yet have you not known me, Philip? He that has seen me has seen the Father."

In this conversation Jesus promised, "If you shall ask anything in my name, I will do it." He also promised the Holy Ghost; He said, "If you love me keep my commandments, and I will pray the Father and He shall give you another comforter that he may abide with you forever. I will not leave you comfortless." As Jesus continued to talk to his disciples, he said, "I am the true vine and my Father is the husbandman." This means, my friends, that in Jesus there is life, pardon, peace, power, provision, companionship, hope, truth, assurance, joy, heaven, and love. He goes on with, "Every branch in me that bears not fruit he takes away; and every branch that bears fruit he purges it that it may bring forth more fruit."

Now, let us see about this fruit. What does he mean by "Every branch in me that bears not fruit he takes away?" In the agricultural sense we will use the grape vine as an illustration. During this time the branches of a grape vine which failed to bear fruit were considered worthless. In fact, the law forbade that barren vine branches be used even as wood for the altar. Fruitless branches were to be disposed of by burning . Any gardener knows the value of pruning. Un-pruned branches drain strength and energy from the plant. The goal of pruning is a larger production of fruit. So it is in the Christian churches. The unfruitful branches in the choir, the unfruitful branches on the usher board, the unfruitful branches in the ministry, the unfruitful branches in all areas of the Christian churches are draining off the time and energy of our ministers and other leaders thereby restricting the fruit bearing of our churches.

"But every branch that bears fruit he purges it that it may bring forth more fruit." My sisters and my brothers, God wants us to be fruitful so he purges us. That means he cleanses us and gets rid of impurities, foreign matter, or undesirable elements so that we may "bear fruit, more fruit, and much fruit." In order to be most fruitful we must live in union with Christ; in this abiding union we can bear fruit. The word "abide" indicates staying, living, dwelling, continuing, persisting, and remaining. Without us abiding in Christ, we can do nothing. I am; you are; abide in me. After Jesus finished instructing His disciples, he lifted up his eyes to heaven and prayed saying, "Father the hour is come, glorify your Son that your Son may glorify you" (17:1). As Jesus prayed, he said, "I pray not that you should take them out of the world, but that you should keep them from the evil" (vs.15).

When Jesus had finished praying, he went to the garden. A band of men and officers came and took him away. They crucified him; they laid him in the tomb. He laid there like a man, but on the third day he rose up like the God that he was. He was seen of them forty days speaking of things pertaining to the Kingdom of God. Then early one morning, after being assembled together with them, Jesus told them not to "depart from Jerusalem, but wait for the promise of the Father, which you have heard of me. For John truly baptized with water; but you shall be baptized with the Holy Ghost not many days hence" (Acts 1:4-5). Then a cloud appeared; Jesus stepped on board. He had already told them to "remember me" and assured them that "I'll be with you always even to the end of the world" (Matthew 28:20). He moved on up; He had told them, "I am, you are, abide in me."

WOMEN'S DAY THEMES

WOMEN GIVING THEIR ALL TO CHRIST

I Samuel 1:15-19, 21-28

Key Verses: I Samuel 1:15, 26-28 - *And Hannah answered and said, No my lord, I am a woman of a sorrowful spirit: I have drunk neither wine nor strong drink, but have poured out my soul before the Lord. [. . .]. And she said, Oh my lord, as your soul lives, my lord, I am the woman that stood by you here, praying unto the Lord. For this child I prayed; and the Lord has given me my petition which I asked of him: Therefore also I have lent him to the Lord; as long as he lives he shall be lent to the Lord. And he worshipped the Lord there.*

In the scriptures for today, we find the story about a woman named Hannah. The name Hannah means gracious or favor. In Biblical days names often carried special meanings. In the story we find that Hannah was married to a man named Elkanah who was from a good family and provided well for his wife. As in most marriages there are some problems. How can there be problems in what sounds like a good marriage? Here's a man that's from a good family and a good provider; what's the problem? Well problem number one was that Hannah had no children. Problem number two was that Hannah's husband Elkanah had another wife named Peninnah; she had children. My, my, these are problems: two wives in the same household, one with children, the other childless.

Let us look at how Hannah dealt with the problem and if she lived up to the meaning of her name. We find that every year Elkanah would take his wives and children up to Shiloh to worship and sacrifice unto the Lord of hosts. Let's pause a moment to talk about the Lord of hosts then we will get back to the story about Hannah. In Old Testament times we find that the people who prayed had many different names for God. These names were according to whatever the need. In Hebrew, Lord of hosts is Jehovah Sabaoth. Lord = Jehovah; Sabaoth = hosts. This is with special reference to warfare or service. In use, the two ideas are united; Jehovah is the Lord of warrior hosts; therefore, it is the name of the Lord in manifestation of power. So, in God's redemptive relation to man, various compound names of Jehovah are used to reveal God as meeting every need of man from his lost state to the end. To sum it all up, the word "hosts" in the Bible is related to heavenly bodies, angels, saints, and sinners. As Lord of hosts God is able to order all of these hosts to fulfill His purpose and to help His people. Thus, we find Elkanah going up to worship and sacrifice unto the Lord of hosts, the King of glory.

Now, let's get back to the story. Ladies, here we find Hannah trying to worship and sacrifice to the Lord of hosts and couldn't do such a good job because her adversary, Peninnah, provoked her relentlessly. You know how it is, as long as you are just sitting around working puzzles, looking at television, and playing Solitaire, nothing happens, but the minute you try to do something for God, up comes the devil. Peninnah provoked Hannah to the point of tears and loss of her appetite. Her husband asked her why she was weeping, wouldn't eat, and was so grieved. It hurt his feelings that here he was with all of his good credentials, and she was crying and not eating because she didn't have a child. He asked her, "Am I not better to you than ten sons?" Elkanah just didn't understand. To Hannah, in Biblical days, barrenness was considered a sign of God's displeasure, and Elkanah could do nothing to erase from Hannah's heart the grief of feeling rejected by God.

Ladies, I greatly admire Hannah. One of the things I admire about her is that she had no insecurities about her husband even though he had another wife. All Hannah wanted was a male child. Where did Hannah go, and what did she do to find relief from the pressures of being childless with the other wife tormenting her to tears and loss of her appetite? I'll tell you what she did. Hannah went to the temple where God and God's man, the priest Eli were. God emphatically stated in Matthew 18:20, "For where two or three are gathered together in my name there am I in the midst of them." So, God was there; Eli was there; and Hannah was there. In going to the temple to pray alone, Hannah broke the laws of custom because she was heartbroken. True prayer is essentially conversation with God. It is not limited by set forms, places, times, postures or words. Hannah just wanted to pray to the Lord of hosts; she poured out her heart to Him. She did as Philippians 4:6 tells us, "Be careful for nothing, but in everything by prayer and supplication with thanksgiving, let your requests be made known unto God." Yes, my friends, Hannah worshipped and sacrificed to God. She prayed to God being specific about what she wanted. She was not wishy-washy like just saying all I want is a baby; she said that she wanted a male child.

Hannah was a giving woman. She vowed a vow to God that if He would give her a man child, "I will give him unto God all the days of his life and that no razor shall come upon his head" (vs. 11). Hannah's promise to God about not cutting this son's hair, the son that she didn't have yet, was the vow of a Nazarite, an outward sign that he was set apart for the Lord. Hannah was patient, thankful, honest, and faithful, for she waited patiently until God answered her prayer and gave her a son. She gave thanks in her song found in Chapter 2 of I Samuel. After her son Samuel was weaned, she took him to the temple and lent him to the Lord all the days of his life. She did not abandon him. Every year she made clothes and would take them to her son Samuel who grew up to be one of the earliest Hebrew prophets after Moses and the last of the judges before the kings began. As reward for her prayer and obedience, God gave her three more sons and two daughters. God gave His Son; they called Him Jesus which means "Jehovah is salvation." Hannah gave her son; she called him Samuel which means asked of God. The moral of this story is that we can never sacrifice anything precious to God but that He gives us something far better in return.

We, as women giving our all to Christ, may have to do like Hannah. Sometimes we may have to cry and lose our appetite for food, but let us not let the trials cause us to rebel and accuse God of injustice and develop into bitter, cold, shriveled souls. We have a standing invitation from Hebrews 4:16, "Let us come boldly unto the throne of grace that we may obtain mercy, and find grace to help in time of need." Yes, since we have this faith and since we have this hope, ladies, as we enter the 21st Century, there is much work to be done for ourselves and then for others. Since this wonderful change has come over us, we must no longer be carnal minded but spiritual minded, and as such, we must eat spiritual food. I Corinthians 10:3-4 tell us, "And did eat the same spiritual meat; and did all drink the same spiritual drink; for they drank of that Spiritual Rock that followed them and that Rock was Christ." John 6:32, 35 tells us that God gives us true bread from heaven and that Bread is Jesus, the Bread of life.

Along with our spiritual food is our spiritual exercise; you know diet and exercise go together if you want to get good results. In our spiritual exercise we are to:

- Walk - have good conduct; Ephesians 4:1-6; Galatians 5:16;
- Run - be fervent, not slothful; Hebrews 12:1;
- Press - exert or push ourselves; Philippians 3:14;
- Wrestle - give it all you got; Eph. 6:12;
- Fight - use the word of God; I Timothy 6:12;
- Work - doing good; Matthew 21:26;
- War - use all of your armor and your resources which include prayer; II Tim. 2:3-5;
- Put off - shed the old [woman] and her deeds;
- Put on - the new "woman".

When we do these things daily for ourselves by the aid of the Holy Spirit, we grow. These things help prepare us to become better women giving our all to Christ.

Yes, my friends, as women giving our all to Christ, I want you to know that one of the greatest assets that we, as women, have is our influence. It has been stated that the hands that rock the cradle rule the world. More than that, beside every good man was and is a good wife, mother, grandmother, aunt, or sister. Woman may inspire to great heights or drag to the lowest depth, but the godly woman's influence flows from her Christ-controlled personality, and she recognizes her influence as a gift from God to be used for His glory and honor.

Yes, "He (God) has blessed us with all spiritual blessings in heavenly places in Christ: according as He has chosen us in Him before the foundation of the world, that we should be holy and without blame before Him in love" (Eph. 1:3b-4). Ladies, we "are a chosen generation, a royal priesthood, an holy nation, a people of His own" (I Peter 2:9). Since we know this, we have this blessed assurance that whatever happens to us while we are giving our all to Christ, "God is our refuge and strength, a very present help in trouble" (Psalm 46:1). We have this trust, and we can ask, "May our sons in their youth be like plants that grow up strong; May our daughters be like corner stones which adorn the corners of a palace; May our barns be filled with crops of every kind; May the sheep in our fields bear young by the tens of thousands; May our cattle produce plentifully without losing any; May there be no complaining in our streets" (Ps. 144:12-14, *English Version*).

Yes, we have a lot of work that needs to be done, for, you see, the world is hungry for the living Bread, and we should lift the Savior up for them to see. We've got to tell the world that the wages of sin is death; the gift of God is eternal life/salvation. We've got to tell it; we've got to excel in it; we've got to pray it in, and we've got to work it out. All in all, the key word is obedience. When we fail to obey, it means that we are not following God's Word, the Holy Scriptures, which was "given by inspiration of God and is profitable for doctrine, for reproof, for correction, for instruction in righteousness that the (woman) of God may be perfect thoroughly furnished unto all good works" (II Timothy 3:16-17). Then, and only then, will we be able to answer to God's call and respond to social issues such as drugs, alcohol, abortion, prostitution, and all of Satan's vices. We have the Word of God on this, that, "One shall chase a thousand and two put ten thousand to flight" (Deuteronomy 32:30). "The Lord our God, he it is who fights for [us], as he has promised [us]" (Joshua 23:10).

Ladies, we bid farewell to Hannah and to all women found in God's ancient portrait gallery. It is with a sense of gratitude to God for giving us so many who shine as bright illustrations of all that is so noble in woman. My own life has been enriched through a closer acquaintance with them. There are others like Delilah the destroyer and Jezebel the murderess that we shall not meet in heaven unless in their last moments they lifted up their hearts in penitence to Him who said, "Whosoever call upon the name of the Lord shall be saved" (Acts 2:21). What rapture will thrill our souls when in a fairer paradise; we gaze upon the glorified bodies of these great women:

- Eve, the first woman who ever cast her smile over the lonely path of man;
- Sarah, the mother of the faithful;

- Racheal, no longer weeping over her children, but rejoicing in their eternal bliss;

- Ruth, her arms full of golden sheaves;

- Hannah, bowing before the eternal throne with her famous son, Samuel;

- Elisabeth and Mary, blessed above women, engaging in sweet conversation and worshipping Him to whom they were related on earth;

- The Elect Lady, with her children around, lost in wonder as they constantly look upon Him who came as "The Truth"; and

- Biblical female saints and women of all ages who loved the Savior and ministered unto Him of their substance. They will form a large part of the ever-expanding circle of the redeemed and join in with the song which the angels cannot sing-- "Unto Him that loved us and washed us from our sins in His own blood, and has made us kings and priests unto God and His Father, to Him be glory and dominion forever and ever" (Revelation 5b-6).

For ourselves it is sufficient to know that whether our names are known abroad or unknown, easy or difficult to pronounce, short or long, full of meaning or unattractive, they are written upon God's palms, and in heaven every child of His is to have a new name (Isaiah 49:15, Rev. 2:17). Finally, as in the words of a song, "A charge to keep I have, a God to glorify,/ A never dying soul to save and fit it for the sky./ To serve the present age, my calling to fulfill/ O, may it all my powers engage to do my Master's will." Thank you.

THE CHOSEN WOMAN

John 15:15-16

John 15:15-16 - *"Henceforth I call you not servants; for the servant knows not what his lord does: but I have called you friends; for all things that I have heard of my Father I have made known unto you. You have not chosen me, but I have chosen you, and ordained you that you should go and bring forth fruit, and that your fruit should remain: that whatsoever you shall ask of the Father in my name, he may give it you.*

The writer of these inspired words was John, the disciple whom Jesus loved (John 21:20-24). It was written after his return from exile in Patmos for the purpose as stated in John 20:31, "But these are written, that you might believe that Jesus is the Christ, the Son of God; and that believing, you might have life through His name." John presents Christ as the Son of God (1:34, 49) who was sent from God (3:2; 6:46) and always spoke the message God gave him (3:34; 7:16-17).

The setting is the Upper Room where Jesus had met with his disciples on the Passover eve. They had eaten the Supper. Jesus had sent Judas, the traitor, away and had washed the disciples' feet. Now He begins to prepare the eleven for His coming death and resurrection. Jesus is comforting His disciples before He leaves. He tells them in the 14th chapter, "Let not your hearts be troubled: you believe in God believe also in me." As Jesus continues to talk He said in the 15th chapter, "I am the true vine and my Father is the husbandman." Women, this means that in Jesus there is life, pardon, peace, power, provision, companionship, hope, truth, assurance, joy, heaven, and love. Jesus goes on by saying, "Every branch in me that bears not fruit He takes away." This means that if we as believers in Christ do not mend our ways or as the young people say, clean up our act, God will either warn us, chastise us, or just take us out of the world. Now, "Every branch that bears fruit, He purges it, that it may bring forth more fruit." This means that the Father cleanses the branches by removing things from our lives that hinder fruitfulness, and we know that we are cleansed through the Word because John 15:3 says so.

As I fore stated, our scripture for today says, "I call you not servants for the servant knows not what his lord does: but I have called you friends; for all things that I have heard of my Father I have made known unto you. You have not chosen me, but I have chosen you, that you should go and bring forth fruit and that your fruit should remain; that whatever you shall ask of the Father in my name, He may give it you." Our theme is "The Chosen Woman." The word "chosen" means selected or marked for favor or special privilege; elect (carefully selected; chosen); chosen for eternal life through divine mercy; or chosen for office or position but not yet installed (president elect). The word "ordained" means to set, place, order, or establish.

There are many chosen in the Bible. To name a few, there are the Israelites who were a chosen people. Deuteronomy 7:6 says, "For you are an holy people unto the Lord your God; the Lord your God hath chosen you to be a special people unto himself above all people who are upon the face of the earth." Jerusalem was chosen as the seat of the temple (I Kings 11:13). Christ was chosen (elect), (Isaiah 2:1) of God to be the Savior of men." The apostles were chosen of God to be witnesses of the resurrection (Acts 10:41). We, the born again believers in Christ, are as I Peter 2:9 says, "But you are a chosen generation, a royal priesthood, an holy nation, a people of his own, that you should show forth the praises of him who has called you out of darkness into his marvelous light."

My sisters and brothers, we should be leaping, shouting, and praising God, for it is an honor to be chosen by God, not only chosen, but also ordained for the purpose of serving Him. For the Scriptures declare in Matthew 22:14, "Many are called, but few chosen." God did not save us to sit down; He called us into His service. This call is not based on any dependence on us; it rests on His love and grace. His call carries with it the promise that He will be with us and will enable us to do His commands. This promise provides us with the confidence to answer His call. As we respond to God's call, we may expect Him to show us step by step the work He wants us to do for Him.

The work, or should I say fruit, may be converts (Romans 1:13), Christian character which is called the fruit of the Spirit (Galatians 5:22-23), or conduct which is called the fruit of righteousness (Rom. 6:21-22; Philippians 1:11). Yes, the only way that we can continue to bear fruit is to be constantly exposed to the teaching of the Word. Where there is no study and application of the Scriptures there will be no fruit; however, if these things are done, there will be more fruit. Not only will there be more fruit, but as we abide in Christ, He also told us in the last sentence of our theme scripture, "[. . .] whatever you shall ask of the Father in my name, he may give it you." This is on the condition that we continue to abide in Him, His words abide in us, and in being absolutely willing to obey God. Then we can say as David in Psalm 37:4, "Delight yourself also in the Lord: And he shall give you the desires of your heart." When we do this, God is able to transform our desires by His word so that we ask according to His will. Christ has assured us that when we do according to His words, the Father is glorified in us, and we shall be His disciples.

Isn't it sweet just to know that we, the saved, are in union with God, the one who made the world and all things therein? Isn't it sweet just to know "[. . .] that all things work together for good to them that love God, to them who are the called according to his purpose" (Rom. 8:28)? Isn't it sweet just to know that, "For the children being not yet born, neither having done any good or evil, that the purpose of God according to election might stand, not of works, but of him that calls" (Rom. 9:10)? Isn't it sweet just to know that God added in verse 25, "I will call them my people who were not my people and her beloved who was not beloved"?

My friends, besides knowing all of these things, God told us the world's attitude towards believers in Christ. He said in verses 18-19, "If the world hates you, you know that it hated me before it hated you. If you were of the world the world would love its own; but because you are not of the world, but I have chosen you out of the world; therefore the world hates you." Do you know why I love about the Lord? He doesn't leave you wondering which way to go or what to do. In John 16:33 Jesus said, "These things have I spoken unto you, that in me you might have peace, In the world you shall have tribulations, but be of good cheer; I have overcome the world." Yes, my friends, as the commercial once said, "Ain't nothing like the real thing;" Jesus is the real thing. All we have to do is keep trusting, keep right on believing; there will be a brighter day.

The Psalmist said in the 37th division which begins, "Fret not yourself because of evildoers, neither be envious against the workers of iniquity, for they shall soon be cut down like the grass, and wither as the green herb" (vs.1-2). You need to read it all when you get time. Along the way verses 12-13 says, "The wicked plots against the just, and gnashes upon him with his teeth, The Lord shall laugh at him: for he sees that his day is coming." Did you know that the Lord can laugh? Verses 15-17 says, "Their sword shall enter into their own heart, and their bows shall be broken. A little that a righteous man has is better than the riches of many wicked. For the arms of the wicked shall be broken: but the Lord upholds the righteous."

I am trying not to read it all, but verses 23-24 adds, "The steps of a good man are ordered by the Lord; and he delights in his way, Though he fall, he shall not be utterly cast down; for the Lord upholds him with his hand;" and you thought you were in good hands with All-State. Verses 34-37 advises us to "Wait on the Lord, and keep his way, and he shall exalt you to inherit the land: when the wicked are cut off, you shall see it. I have seen the wicked in great power, and spreading himself like a green bay tree. Yet he passed away, and, lo, he was not; yea, I sought him, but he could not be found. Mark the perfect man, and behold the upright: for the end of that man is peace." The psalm ends with verses 39-40, "But the salvation of the righteous is of the Lord; he is their strength in the time of trouble. And the Lord shall help them, and deliver them: he shall deliver them from the wicked, and save them, because they trust him."

No wonder the song writer wrote, "What a fellowship; what a joy divine leaning on the everlasting arm." I'm so glad that the Lord saved me; yes, I'm glad about it. God has given me his Word and the testimony of Jesus Christ. He has given me a new song to sing; I've been redeemed. He has given me to know the life of Jesus--the solitary life of a young man who was born in a small village, the child of a peasant woman who grew up and worked in a carpenter shop until He was thirty. Then, for three years he traveled from place to place preaching. God has given me to know that He never wrote a book; He never held an office; He never owned a home; He never had a wife and children; He never went to college; He never put His foot inside a big city; He never traveled more that 200 miles from the place where he was born; He never did any of the things that usually accompany greatness; and He had no credentials but Himself. Yet, while he was still a young man most of the public opinion turned against Him; His friends ran away. He was turned over to His enemies who put Him through the mockery of a trial. He was nailed to a cross and hung between two thieves. While he was dying, His executioners gambled for the only piece of property He had on earth, His coat. When He was dead, He was laid in a borrowed tomb through the pity of a friend. Twenty centuries have come and gone, but today He is the central figure of the human race, and the leader of the supporting pillar of progress. I can truly say that all the armies that have ever marched, all the navies that have ever sailed, all the parliaments that have ever sat, and all the kings that have ever reigned put together have not affected the life of man upon earth as has that "One Solitary Life" (paraphrased, Anonymous)

Yes my friends God is the joy and strength of my life. He moves all pain, misery, and strife. I want to go with Him when He comes back; I've come too far and I'll never turn back. Do you know why? God is my all and all? Thank you.

STEPS TO THE CHRISTIAN LIFE: COME, COMMIT, CONTINUE

(Various Scriptures)

The World Book Dictionary says that the word "come" means to happen, take place, occur or to be available. It expresses action, being, occurrence, etc. It is also in the imperative mood which is used to give commands or to make requests and means not to be avoided; it's urgent; it's necessary here in this life. The first mention of the word "come" in regards to our salvation is found in Genesis 7:1 where God extended an invitation to Mr. & Mrs. Noah and Family saying, "Come, you and all your house, into the ark." This gracious invitation occurs again and again in the Scriptures, even down to the last page, "And the Spirit and the bride say, Come. And let him that hears say, Come. And him that is athirst come. And whosoever will let him take the water of life freely" (Revelation 22:17). Notice that this invitation is extended by God to man; it urges man to avail himself to the perfect provision God has made for his preservation, and it is given in a time of overwhelming judgment and doom.

My friends, I thank God for the standing invitation. Down through the ages God is still saying, "Come". If we read Isaiah 55:1, 3, the invitation says, "Ho, everyone that thirsts, come to the waters, and he that has no money; come, buy and eat; yea, come, buy wine and milk without money and without price. [. . .] Incline your ear, and come unto me; hear, and your soul shall live." Yes, in spite of all of our misbehaving, God is not willing that any should perish, but that all should come to repentance. He stands ready, willing, and able. In Isaiah 1:18 the record says, "Come now, and let us reason together; though your sins be as scarlet, they shall be as white as snow; though they be red like crimson, they shall be as wool."

My friends, in order to come to God there are some stipulations. Notice the spiritual part. Acts 17:28 says, "For in him we live, and move, and have our being." This tells me that we cannot do *a* thing, *any*thing, or *no*thing without God. If God had not breathed into man's nostrils the breath of life, man would still be just a form. Sometimes we even go so far as to make statements like, "I'll do it myself." I want you to know today that this is God's world. I beg to differ with the singer James Brown who sang that it's a man's world, not so. This is God's world and everything in it even down to our salvation. So the spiritual stipulations are:

1. Acts 17:28: "For in him we live, and move, and have our being."
2. John 6:44: "No man can come to me except the Father (God) who has sent me, draw him."
3. John 15:16: "You have not chosen me, but I have chosen you."
4. Mark 4:16: "Come after me, and I will make you become {. . .}."

These are the spiritual stipulations, but your part is as stated in Hebrews 11:6, "But without faith it is impossible to please him; for he that comes to God must believe that he is." Our part also includes Romans 10:17, "So then, faith comes by hearing and hearing by the word of God."

Ladies, I honor the woman of Samaria who, when Jesus was in the city, had faith enough in him to leave her water pot and her prejudices, "[. . .] went her way into the city, and said to the men, come, see a man who told me all things that ever I did" (John 4:28-29). This allowed her to find the path to personal wholeness and to be a blessing to others. Yes, ladies, the invitation to "come" is still open as Revelation 22:17 tells us.

The second step to the Christian life is "Commit". The word "commit" means to hand over for safe keeping, to put in charge or trust, obligate, bind, or to pledge or assign to some particular course or use. Jesus said in Matthew 16:24, "If any man will come after me, let him deny himself, and take up his cross, and follow me." Now, that's kind of hard for some of us to do. Most of us don't want commitments; we don't want responsibilities to God or man. We just want to do our own thing. We don't want anything to tie us down, but God has not changed his word. He is still saying, "If any man will [. . .]." Psalm 37:5 tells us, "Commit your way unto the Lord; trust also in him, and he shall bring it to pass." Proverbs 16:3 says, "Commit your works unto the Lord, and your thoughts shall be established."

Ladies, in the second part of our theme, "Steps to the Christian Life", we find that committed women have played and still do play important parts in society, history, and in God's plan. Let us look at Eve. Most men and even some women blame Eve for the mess that we are in today, but the Scriptures say in Romans 5:12, "Wherefore as by **one man** sin entered into the world . . ." However, after all is said and done, God chose Eve to be the mother of all human beings. From Eve we learn that our commitment is *under* our God, *beside* our husbands, and *before* our children in order to bring glory to God in all of our relationships.

Another committed woman was Mary, the mother of our Lord and Savior Jesus Christ, who ushered in a new era in feminine history. While all womankind was represented by Eve, Mary introduced the amazing truth that women are important as individuals. It was many years before the value of woman's mission was recognized as being equal with that of man's mission. The significance of Miriam and Deborah, who were chosen by God for their tasks, is often overlooked or severely understated. I can imagine in my mind that Mary probably prayed and thanked her God daily for giving her a part in God's greatest miracle and for letting her live to see it reenacted in her days. Every time Mary saw Jesus, her baby, being invited into the life of a James or John, a beggar, a sinful woman or a Roman soldier, it happened: Jesus, Mary's baby, enters into another human body to live and move about, not just for nine months, but for life. This committed woman, Mary, let us know that we are to yield ourselves to God--body, mind, emotions-- so that through us Jesus can show the world what He is like.

Let us look at the woman called the Virtuous Woman found in Proverbs 31. The Bible does not give a name; it just describes a committed woman as told to King Lemuel by his mother who was teaching her son not to be foolish. Lemuel's mother taught him not to give his strength to a strange woman. She also taught him that a good woman is hard to find. She goes on to tell him what a good, committed woman will do. Verse 11 says, "The heart of her husband does safely trust in her, so that he shall have no need of spoil. This woman has many virtues. She is strong in wisdom, grace, and in the fear of God. This woman is a chaste, trustworthy, business woman. This woman, as we say, "has everything going for her." She deals honorably with her husband, her children, and all others, but above all, she fears God. Men, when you find a good wife, hold on to her, love, and cherish her, and you won't have to go around asking anybody, "Have you seen my wife?"

Ladies, not only can we be committed, but we also can be very influential. Yes ladies what a wonderful change in our life has been wrought since Jesus came into our heart. I want you to know that one of the greatest assets that we women have is our influence. Woman has a unique way of leaving the imprint of her character and words upon every life that she touches. She may inspire to great heights or drag to the lowest depths. It has been said that the hand that rocks the cradle rules the world. So, women, as godly women, let us use our influence as a gift from God for His glory and honor. If we do, we can say just as our Savior, Jesus Christ, "Into your hand I commit my spirit" (Ps. 31:5).

The third and final step to the Christian life is "Continue". The word "continue" means to go; keep up; keep on; to go on after stopping; to last; endure; to stay; or to remain in a certain way. My friends, we have come this far by faith, leaning on the Lord, trusting in His Holy Word, and He's never failed us yet. As Hebrews 6:1 tells us, "Therefore leaving the principles of the doctrine of Christ, let us go on to perfection" (maturity). Some of us never get out of the I-know-I've-been-born-again stage.

But, let us step on up to Jesus for we are in the army now, God's army. We have been inducted into the service of the Lord. We have had our basic training and are fully committed to the cause of Christ. Now we are being given instructions in how to be able to continue in the service of the Lord. We have been forewarned, and that means we are forearmed. Yes, God lets us know in Romans 8:31 that "If God is for us, who can be against us?" Joshua 23:10 says, "One man of you shall chase a thousand; for the Lord your God, he it is who fights for you, as he promised." Ladies and gentlemen, we have been instructed to be "wise as serpents and harmless as doves" (Matt. 10:16).

Ephesians 6:10-12 tells us that we should "Be strong in the Lord and in the power of His might. Put on the whole armor of God that we may be able to stand against the wiles of the devil. For we are not fighting a flesh and blood battle, but against principalities, against powers, against the rulers of the darkness of this world, against spiritual wickedness." As soldiers in God's army, we know that the task that lies ahead is full of pitfalls, detours, and hardships. We also know that the devil and all of his demons are out to delay us, trip us up, and sift us as wheat. But, we are going to be using our resource, and that is, "Praying with all prayer and supplication in the spirit, and watching with all perseverance and supplication for all saints" (vs. 18).

We are to use what we have received from the Lord to resist sin and Satan and to render our due benevolence unto the Lord. We are to "continue in the faith, grounded and settled, and be not moved away from the hope of the gospel which you have heard" (Colossians 1:23). We are to be "steadfast, unmovable, always abounding in the work of the Lord" (I Cor. 15:58). "Being confident of this very thing, that he who has begun a good work in you will perform it until the day of Jesus Christ" (Phil. 1:6). Thank you.

WOMEN CHOSEN BY GOD
TO DO GOOD WORKS

Ephesians 2:10

Ephesians 2:10 – *For we are his workmanship, created in Christ Jesus unto good works, which God has before ordained that we should walk in them.*

A few days ago I was reading a local newspaper and saw where there were ten Women of Achievement who were soon to be announced. These women would be honored for their contributions to the community in the areas of Health Concerns, Cultural Enrichment, Communications, Civic Betterment, Social Responsibility, Business and Community, Community Service, Volunteer Service, Education, and Youth Welfare. They would become a part of a group of previously honored Women of Achievement over the last 33 years. Out of all these good achievements named, there was no mention of Women of Achievement in the category of The Cause For Christ. There was no mention of the outstanding women who were chosen by God to do good works; they were not to be included with any previously chosen women, so tonight we will give honor to whom honor is due. Thinking on the scripture written in Ephesians 2:10, "For we are his workmanship, created in Christ Jesus unto good works, which God has before ordained that we should walk in them," an appropriate topic emerged: "Women Chosen by God To Do Good Works."

As women chosen by God, I thought it fitting to mention some chosen women of the Bible. Naturally Mother Eve came to mind. Regardless of what has been said about her, no one can take from her the fact that she was the first woman and that she was chosen by God to be the mother of all human beings to come. We learn from Mother Eve that woman's place is under her God, beside her husband, and before her children bringing a glory to God in all of her relationships. Another woman of the Bible chosen by God was Mary, the mother of our Lord and Savior Jesus Christ. Through Mary we learn that woman's mission in life is to yield herself to God --body, mind, emotions--so that through her God can show the world what He is like.

There are many other women in the Bible like Miriam of whom God Himself spoke in Micah 6:4, "For I brought you out of the land of Egypt, and redeemed you out of the house of servants; and I sent before you Moses, Aaron, and Miriam." These Biblical women were chosen by God to do a good work, but time does not permit me to speak about all of them. For now, I will speak about all of us women and girls here today who have also been chosen by God to do a good work. Women, I want you to know today that we were not chosen because of some great achievements like the women in the newspaper. Scripture tells us that "many are called but few are chosen" (Matt. 12:14). "There is none that understands; there is none that seeks after God" (Rom. 3:11). "It is by grace that [we] are saved through faith, and that not of [ourselves], it is the gift of God--not of works lest any man should boast. For, we are his workmanship, created in Christ Jesus unto good works, which God has before ordained that we should walk in them." Women, I feel good in knowing that God has chosen us; we didn't choose Him for Scriptures say, "You have not chosen me, but I have chosen you, and ordained you, that you should go and bring forth fruit" (John 15:16). "For we are laborers together with God; you are God's cultivated field, you are God's building" (I Corinthians 3:9).

Yes, we have been chosen by God; we belong to God. We have been purchased by the precious blood of Jesus. We were slaves to sin. We all know that the cost of freedom has always been high, but Jesus paid it all. Now that Jesus has set us free, there is much to be done for ourselves and then for others. Since this great transformation, we should no longer be carnal minded, but spiritual minded, and as spiritual beings, we must eat spiritual food. I Corinthians 10:3-4 say, "And did all eat the same spiritual meat; and did all drink the same spiritual drink; for they drank of that spiritual Rock that followed them: and that Rock was Christ." God also gave us the true Bread from heaven, for Jesus declared, "I am the Bread of Life" (John 6:35).

Along with our spiritual diet is our spiritual exercise. We have to change into our exercise clothes and then proceed. We are to:

- <u>Put off</u> the old man with his deeds; And [. . .] <u>put on</u> the new man which is renewed in knowledge after him that created him, Colossians 3:9b-10.

- <u>Wash</u> your heart from wickedness, Jeremiah 4:14.

- <u>Work</u> today in my vineyard, Matthew 21:28.

- <u>Work</u> out your own salvation with fear and trembling. For it is God which works in you both to will and to do of his good pleasure, Philippians 2:12b-13.

- <u>Walk</u> in the Spirit, Galatians 5:16.

- <u>Walk</u> worthy of the vocation wherewith you are called,, With all lowliness and meekness, with longsuffering, forbearing one another in love; Endeavoring to keep the unity of the Spirit in the bond of peace, Eph. 4:1-6.

- <u>Wrestle</u> [. . .] against powers, against the rulers of the darkness of this world, against spiritual wickedness in high places, Eph. 6:12.

- <u>Press</u> toward the mark for the prize of the high calling of God in Christ Jesus, Phil. 3:14.

- <u>Fight</u> the good fight of faith, I Timothy 6:12.

- <u>War</u>: Endure hardness as a good soldier of Jesus Christ. No man that <u>wars</u> entangles himself with the affairs of this life; that he may please him who has chosen him to be a soldier, II Timothy 2:3-4.

- <u>Run</u> with patience the race that is set before us, Hebrews 12:1.

- Sometimes we might even have to just <u>Stand</u> fast therefore in the liberty where with Christ has made us free, and be not entangled again with the yoke of bondage, (Gal. 5:1); "and having done all, <u>stand</u>, Eph. 6:13b.

We should do these things daily whereby we grow and are further prepared to do good works.

As women chosen by God, I want you to know that one of the greatest assets that we have is our influence. It has been said that the hand that rocks the cradle rules the world. Woman has a unique way of leaving the imprint of her character and words upon every life she touches; she may inspire to great heights or drag to the lowest depth. The godly woman's influence flows from her Christ-controlled personality, and she recognizes her influence as a gift from God to use for His glory and honor. Yes, "God has blessed us with all spiritual blessings in heavenly places in Christ: according as he has chosen us in him before the foundation of the world, that we should be holy and without blame before him in love" (Eph. 1:3b-4).

Ladies, since we know that we are "a chosen generation, a royal priesthood, an holy nation, a people of his own" (I Peter 2:9), we have this assurance that whatever happens while we are on this Christian journey and doing our Christian duties, " God is our refuge and strength, a very present help in trouble, therefore will not we fear, though the earth be removed, and though the mountains be carried into the midst of the sea" (Psalm 46:1-2). We have this trust, "That our sons may be as plants grown up in their youth; that our daughters may be like cornerstones" (144:12). We also pray, "Send out your light and your truth; let them lead me" (43:3).

Yes, we have a lot of work that needs to be done, for you see the world is hungry for the living Bread , and we should lift the Savior up for them to see. We've got to tell men, women, boys, and girls that the wages of sin is death and the gift of God, eternal life. We've got to tell it, excel in it, pray it in, and work it out. Then, when we put on our war clothes, we will not only be able to defend ourselves but fight against drugs, alcohol, abortion, prostitution, and all of Satan's vices. We have the Word of God on this, for He told us, "One man of you shall chase a thousand; for the Lord your God, he it is who fights for you, as he has promised you" (Joshua 23:10).

My friends, our names might not ever get in the *News Journal, Post Dispatch, New York Times,* or any paper or magazine for some great achievements that we have accomplished, but one thing I'm sure of, and that is if we continue to be faithful, "He who has begun a good work in you will perform it until the day of Jesus Christ" (Philippians 1:6). We can rejoice because our names are written in heaven, and we will be rewarded by God for all of the good works that we have done. Thank you.

SERVICE, A SURE FOUNDATION

Men and Women's Day - I Timothy 6:19

I Timothy 6:19 -*Laying up in store for themselves a good foundation against the time to come, that they may lay hold on eternal life.*

We find that the word "service" means spiritual obedience or useful labor that does not produce a tangible commodity. The word "sure" means certain, fixed, settled, or proved to be true. Foundation is a basic support; something laid down or constructed to serve as a base, or a starting point. Putting this all together, what do we have? In our spiritual service, we are certain that God is the starting point. The reason we know that God is the starting point is found in Genesis 1:1, "In the beginning God [. . .]". So, God is the beginning, the ending, the first and the last. It's for certain that no other foundation can be laid except by God.

When we think of a foundation, we think about building. In building in the natural, the first thing is to lay the foundation. If the foundation is not solid, it will not stand. After a few years it will probably collapse. So, in order to have a foundation that will give good service, you must build it out of rocks, stones, and cement so that when the conditions of time and weather come, it will stand. This is also true spiritually. We must build on the stone, the rejected stone that became the chief corner stone (Psalm 118:22), which is Jesus.

In order to build you must have a mind to build just as the workers on the walls at Jerusalem had. Nehemiah 4:6 says, "So built we the wall for the people had a mind to work." After having a mind to build, let the

Lord help you. Psalm 127:1 says, "Except the Lord build [. . .] they that labor work in vain." While letting the Lord build for us, Satan will try to stop us. We will have to say as the builders on the walls at Jerusalem did in Nehemiah 6:3, "I am doing a great work so that I cannot come down. Why should the work cease, while I leave it and come down." Sometimes we may get tired but Jesus said, "Take my yoke upon you and learn of me; for I am meek and lowly in heart; and you shall find rest unto your souls. For my yoke is easy, and my burden is light" (Matthew 11:29-30).

In order to build we must pray, have faith, hope, and love. We must pray to make known to God our expectations, our hopes, and our aims. We must have faith because without faith it is impossible to please God. We need hope; it is one of the three great Christian virtues. Hope we have as an anchor of the soul, both sure and steadfast. We must have love because God is love, and our faith works by love (Gal. 5:6). Love is what will take us through this world on into eternity. In order to lay hold on eternal life we must let God work in us, and we must do his will. Philippians 2:14-15 tells us that we should also "Do all things without murmuring and disputing, that you may be blameless and harmless, the sons of God without rebuke in the midst of a crooked and perverse nation among whom you shine as lights in the world."

In working on the building, let us be bold, for II Timothy 1:7-9a tells us that, "God has not given us the spirit of fear: but of power, and of love, and of a sound mind. Let us not be ashamed of the testimony of our Lord, [. . .]; who has saved us, and called us with an holy calling [. . .]." People, let us be strong in the grace and "endure hardness as a good soldier" (2:3). Let us "study to show ourselves approved unto God, a workman that needs not to be ashamed {. . .]" (2:15). "Let Christ dwell in your hearts by faith, that you are rooted and grounded in love able to understand [. . .] and be filled with all fullness of God" (Ephesians 3:17-19).

In order to lay up in store for yourself a good foundation, God will not have you to be ignorant, He has made it possible for you to know the way of eternal life and the way of eternal damnation. II Timothy 3:1-7 informs us, "This know also, that in the last days perilous times shall come. For men shall be lovers of their own selves, covetous, boasters, proud, blasphemers, disobedient to parents, unthankful, unholy, without natural affection, truce breakers, false accusers, incontinent, fierce, despisers of those that are good, Traitors, heady, high minded, lovers of pleasure more than lovers of God; Having a form of godliness, but denying the power thereof; from such turn away. [. . .] (They) are ever learning, and never able to come to the knowledge of the truth." We have to put off these things and put on the fruit of the spirit which is in all goodness, righteousness, and truth. Through Christ, we have put them off, but check the list to see if you fit in and are living carnally. "Walk in the spirit and you shall not fulfill the lust of the flesh" (Galatians 5:16).

Now, let us consider a few of the old patriots. I'm sure that if Noah were here, he could testify to the fact that serving God will pay off. Noah could tell you that when God opened up the fountains of the deep and the windows of heaven and let the waters come, he and his family were saved. I'm sure that if Moses were standing here today, he could tell you that the Lord is a man of war. Moses was assured of this because on his great exodus from Egypt, when he came to the point of no return with the Red Sea before him, the wilderness on both sides, and Pharaoh's army bringing up the rear, he and all of Israel were saved. I know that if Jonah could speak today, he would tell you that prayer changes things. After being swallowed by a large fish, he kneeled in prayer, and he was saved.

God not only helped the old patriots, but He also will help us in our old age or in any time of trouble. David testified in the Psalms that God will not forsake the righteous, nor will his seed be begging bread. No wonder the songwriter said, "I'm working on the building; it's a true foundation. I'm holding up the blood-stained banner for my Lord. Just as soon as I get though working on the building, I'm going up to heaven to get my reward."

"Finally, my brethren (and sisters), be strong in the Lord, and in the power of his might. Put on the whole armor of God that you may be able to stand against the wiles of the devil. [. . .] Stand, therefore, having your loins girt about with truth, and having on the breastplate of righteousness; and your feet shod with the preparation of the gospel of peace; taking the shield of faith, wherewith you shall be able to quench all the fiery darts of the wicked. And take the helmet of salvation, and the sword of the spirit which is the word of God: Praying always with all prayer and supplication in the Spirit" (Ephesians 6:10-11, 14-18a). After we have done all of these things and when we get through fighting Satan and his forces, we can say, individually, "I have fought a good fight, I have finished my course, I have kept the faith, Henceforth there is laid up for me a crown of righteousness, which the Lord, the righteous judge shall give me at that day" (II Timothy 4:7-8). Not only can you say these things, but when you cross from time into eternity, you will be able to sing a song that the angels cannot sing: I've been redeemed; I've been washed in the blood. Lay up in store for yourselves a good foundation that you may lay hold on eternal life (see I Timothy 6:19). Amen.

HOLD ON TO YOUR FAITH
IN THE TIME OF CRISIS

II Kings 4:8-9, 18-37 (Edna Y. James)

Key Verses - II Kings 4:8-9, 17-24 - *And it fell on a day, that Elisha passed to Shunem, where was a great woman; and she constrained him to eat bread; And so it was that as oft as he passed by, he turned in there to eat bread. And she said unto her husband, Behold now, I perceive that this is a holy man of God which passes by us continually.*

[. . .] And the woman conceived, and bore a son at that season that Elisha had said unto her, according to the time of life. And when the child was grown, it fell on a day, that he went out to his father to the reapers. And he said unto his father, my head, my head. And he said to a lad, Carry him to his mother. And when he had taken him, and brought him to his mother, he sat on her knees till noon, and then died. And she went up, and laid him on the bed of the man of God, and shut the door upon him, and went out. And she called unto her husband, and said, Send me, I pray thee, one of the young men, and one of the asses, that I may run to the man of God, and come again. And he said, wherefore will you go to him to day? It is neither new moon, nor Sabbath. And she said, It shall be well. Then she saddled an ass, and said to her servant, drive, and go forward; slack not your riding for me, except I bid you.

"Now **faith** is the substance of things hoped for, the evidence of things not seen" (Hebrews 11:1). In today's world "seeing is believing". Biblical faith is believing when you **don't** see it, when you know that you know, or when you know **what** you know, but no one else seems to know. "But without faith, it is impossible to please Him [God]" for he who comes to God must first believe that he **is,** and that He is a rewarder of those who **diligently** seek Him (Heb. 11:6). According to *Strong's Exhaustive Concordance* **diligently** is from the Greek word, exzeteo (ek-zay-teh'-o), to search out, investigate, crave, demand, seek after carefully. This is more than saving faith or straddle-the-fence- sometimes-in-sometimes-out faith only when it is convenient; this is an upgrade, another level in faith, the kind you need when you're facing a crisis.

Crisis, according to the *American Heritage Collegiate Dictionary*, means (1a) a crucial or decisive point or situation, a turning point (b) an unstable condition, as in political affairs, involving an impending abrupt or decisive change. (2). A sudden change in the course of a disease or fever. (3). an emotionally stressful event or traumatic change in a person's life. **Trauma** is a serious injury or shock to the body; an emotional wound that creates substantial lasting damage to the psychological development.

Women, faith, and crisis are not an unusual combination. **Eve,** Adam's rib, or shall I say "prime rib", the best part, slightly marbled with a little more fat to make it extra tender, encountered a crisis, "a crucial or decisive point or situation; a turning point" in the Garden of Eden. This turning point still affects us today, but, yet, she is called the Mother of All Living. She had to "hold on to her faith in the time of crisis."

Jochebed, Moses' mother, encountered a crisis, "an unstable condition [, as] in political affairs [,] involving an impending abrupt or decisive change." The government at the time, President Pharoah, decided to kill all of the male babies. She had to "hold on to her faith in the time of crisis". She is referred to in the Hero Hall of Fame in Hebrews 11:23, "By faith Moses, when he was born, was hidden three months by his parents, because they saw he was a beautiful child; and they were not afraid of the king's command." Diligent faith counteracts fear.

Miriam, Moses' big sister, was always by his side. After all, she was the one who hooked him up with the queen and got his own mother to be the nanny and day-care provider. She was with him as he led the Israelites from bondage. She was a prophetess, but faced a crisis when she got out of her place and spoke against Moses. God became angry with her, but because

Moses intervened, her death sentence was "a sudden change" to the 7-day leprosy disease. The whole nation had to wait until this condition cleared before they made a move. She had to "hold on to her faith in a time of crisis," yet God Himself acknowledged her in Micah 6:4, "For I brought you up from the land of Egypt, I redeemed you from the house of bondage; and I sent before you Moses, Aaron, and **Miriam.**

Then, there were 5 unmarried sisters, **Mahlah, Noah, Hoglah, Milcah, and Tir'zah,** who became very "stressed out" when their father died and left no sons as heirs. They went before the priests, the leaders, and the entire congregation to challenge the inheritance laws. They had to "hold on to their faith in a time of crisis." In Numbers 27:5-7, "Moses brought their case before the Lord, and the Lord spoke to Moses saying, The daughters of Ze.loph'e.had speak what is right; you shall surely give them a possession among their father's brothers, and cause the inheritance of their father to pass to them." Because of them, God proceeds to clarify the inheritance laws. Diligent faith gives boldness.

And then there is the story of the **Shunammite Woman** and her activities summarized from II Kings 4:8-9, 18-26, 27-30:

- Great, notable, married
- Perceptive, discerning- knew **Elisha** was a man of God
1. **Elijah's protégé** - anointed to take Elijah's place; received on-the-job training
2. **Persistent** - would not leave Elijah's side; knew Elijah would be taken
3. **Double portion** - received as promised if he **saw** Elijah taken up.
4. **Proven**- men checked him out to see if he was truthful; searched for Elijah.
- Secure in her faith; when Elisha asked, "What can I do for you?" She wanted nothing.
- Rewarded for her faithfulness- given son in her old age.
- **Faith in crisis** - son died, traumatic situation
1. **Didn't panic**- She was upset, got in a hurry, but didn't panic; knew God is a "very present help in trouble;" didn't snap at her husband; knew it would be alright. Husband accepted her decision.

2. **Sought God first-** didn't go to the funeral home, that was the last option.

3. **Waited on God-** Elisha did not know what was wrong; was compassionate

4. **Was persistent -** accepted no substitute or generic (Everything is not a crisis. Sometime you can call a neighbor, friend, deacon, member of the Mother Board or a parent. You don't have to call the pastor for everything. You can go boldly before the throne of Grace yourself. Diligent faith says you can "ask, seek, and knock and the door shall be opened."

• **Rewarded**

5. **Son raised**

6. **Property restored-** followed Elisha's advice and left because of a 7-year famine; property was taken. Went straight to the King. King was talking with Gehazi, Elisha's assistant, when she walked in. God had already set it up.

Women, when you are going through something, don't let anything or anyone get in the way of you and God. People will tell you, "all that ain't required." They question why you are doing this or going there, "it's not the new moon or the Sabbath." That woman with the issue of blood had been having this hemorrhaging problem for 12 long years. She had to buck the crowd and get to Jesus. What does it take for you to get to Jesus? People ask, "How come you have to raise your hand all of the time?" Well, I'm blessing the Lord like David said in Psalm 63:4, "Thus, will I bless thee while I live: I will lift up my hands in your name." Some want to know, "Why are you always yelling Hallelujah so loud?" When I call on Him, He is near. I know God inhabits the praises of the saints because in Psalm 22:3 David characterizes God, "O you are holy, O you that inhabits the praises of Israel." You see I can't help myself; praise is what I do because I owe Him. He has taken me through crisis after crisis. When I think about God's goodness and all He's done for me, I might raise my hand, yell hallelujah, stand up, make some noise, or whatever it takes for me. What does it require for you to "Hold On To Your Faith in a Time of Crisis? These are times of crises. I heard the choir sing a song that says, "Hold on, be strong, it's only a test."

TALKS

WHO AM I?

Psalm 8:1-6, 9

Psalm 8: 1-6, 9 - *O Lord our Lord, how excellent is your name in all the earth! Who has set your glory above the heavens. Out of the mouth of babes and sucklings have you ordained strength because of your enemies, that you might still the enemy and the avenger. When I consider your heavens, the work of your fingers, the moon and the stars, which you have ordained; what is man, that you are mindful of him? And the son of man, that you visit him? For you have made him a little lower than the angels, and have crowned him with glory and honor. You made him to have dominion over the works of your hands; you have put all things under his feet: [. . .] O Lord our Lord, how excellent is your name in all the earth!*

Who am I? It is the most basic yet deep question a person can ask. It digs at the very meaning of life. Our identities begin forming in infancy. The first stage in the evolution of our self image is the baby's recognition of the familiar -- mother's face, the breast or bottle, the confines of the crib. This stage of development or identity is the **I-am-what-I-am-given** stage. In the second stage, the infant begins to recognize choices and distinguishes between you and me and yours and mine. This formation of the personality is the **I-am-what-I-will** stage.

The child's first true sense of identity comes from trying to imitate his or her parents. In identifying with the parents, the child is demonstrating the first signs of ambition and independence. This is the **I-am-what-I-can-imagine-I-will-be** stage. Upon entering school, the child's identity becomes linked with accomplishments and a feeling of usefulness. As the child learns to earn recognition by producing things, he or she enters the **I-am-what-I-learn** stage.

In adolescence the youth's identity formation relies heavily on group identification. It is the time of cliques and in-crowds. When young people divide themselves into groups with which they can relate, they are in the **I-am-who-I-associate with** stage. With adulthood comes the occupational choices that will be the basis of the grown-up's identity or the **I-am-what-I-do** stage. In later life, the adult's identity revolves around the acceptance of responsibility for the outcome of his or her life known as the **I-am-what-I-have-accomplished stage.** All of the stages of identity development are universal, but the question remains, "Who am I?"

The answer to the question is found in Psalm 8 (read, please). This psalm is a solemn meditation on the glory and greatness of God. It begins and ends with the same acknowledgement of the excellence of God's name; after all, God is the beginning and the ending, the first and the last. For the proof of God's glory, the psalmist gives instances of his goodness to man. God's goodness is his glory as shown in Exodus 33:12-23 where we find Moses' prayer, the Lord's answer, and Moses' new vision for the new task. In verse 18 Moses politely requests of God, "Show me your glory." God answers in verse 19, "And he said, I will make all my goodness pass before you, and I will proclaim the name of the Lord before you; and will be gracious to whom I will be gracious, and will show mercy on whom I will show mercy."

In Psalm 8 God is to be glorified for making known Himself and His great name to us. David greatly admires two things due to God's name. First, in verse 1, how plainly God displays his glory thus inspiring him to proclaim with all humility and reverence that God is his Lord and his people's Lord, "O Lord our Lord." If we believe that God is the Lord, we must admit and acknowledge him to be ours, "O Lord our Lord." The second thing David admires is how powerful God proclaims his glory by the weakest of his creatures. Verse 2 says, "Out of the mouth of babes and sucklings have you ordained strength [. . .]," or what might be called perfected praise. Matthew 21:15-16 says, "And when the chief priests and scribes saw the wonderful things that [Jesus] did, and the children crying in the temple, and saying Hosanna to the Son of David, they were very displeased and said unto Him, Do you hear what these say? And Jesus said unto them; Yea, have you never read (Psalm 8:2), out of the mouth of babes and sucklings you have perfected praise?" This intimates the glory of God.

In the kingdom of nature, God takes care of little children; they are most helpless when they first come into the world. The special protection that they are under and the provisions nature has made for them ought to be acknowledged by every one of us to the glory of God. In the kingdom of grace, the Kingdom of the Messiah, it is here foretold that by the apostles who were looked upon but as babes, unlearned and ignorant men (Acts 4:13), mean and despicable, through the foolishness of their preaching (I Corinthians 1:121), the devil's kingdom should be thrown down as Jericho's walls were by the sound of rams horns.

The gospel is called the arm of the Lord (John 12:38) and the rod of his strength (Revelation 2:27). This was ordained to work wonders, not out of the mouths of philosophers or orators or politicians or statesmen but of a company of poor fishermen. We hear children crying, "Hosanna to the Son of David" when the chief priests and Pharisees owned Him not. Sometimes the grace of God appears wonderfully in young children, and "He teaches them knowledge and make them to understand doctrine, who are but newly weaned from the milk and drawn from the breasts" (Isaiah 28:9). Sometimes the power of God brings to pass great things in His church by very weak and unlikely instruments.

In verses 3-4, the psalmist continues his admiration of God, "When I consider the heavens, the work of your fingers, the moon and the stars which you have ordained; what is man (sinful, weak, miserable man, a creature so forgetful of you and his duty to you) that you are mindful of him? (You take notice of his actions and affairs, and in the making of the world, you have a respect for him.) What is the son of man, that you visit him?" (As one friend visits another, you are pleased to converse with him and concern yourself with him.) In Job 25:6 Job says, "Man is a worm," yet God puts a respect upon him, and shows him abundant kindness; man is above all the creatures in the lower world, the favorite and darling of providence. We may be sure that he takes precedence or priority over all the inhabitants of this lower world, for he is made but "a little lower than the angels" (vs. 5). Lower, indeed, because by his body he is allied to the earth and to the beasts that perish, and yet by his soul, which is spiritual and immortal, he is so near kin to the holy angles that he may be truly said to be but a little lower than they, and is in order next to them. Man is but for a little while lower than the angels while his soul is cooped up in a house of clay, but, never you mind, the children of the resurrection shall be angels' peers (Luke 20:36), and no longer lower than they.

The psalmist is amazed that, "You have crowned him with glory and honor." Man's ability to reason is his crown of glory. God has put all things under man's feet that he might serve himself not only of the labor but of the productions and lives of the inferior creatures. They are all delivered into man's hand; they are all put under man's feet. These verses also refer in a particular manner to Jesus Christ. In Hebrews 2:6-8 the words of the psalmist are repeated and in verse 9 paralleled to Jesus, "But we see Jesus, who was made a little lower than the angels for the sufferings of death, crowned with glory and honor; that he by the grace of God should taste death for every man." Christ assumed the nature of man, and in that nature humbled Himself. He was for a little while made lower than the angels when he took upon himself the form of a servant and made himself of no reputation. In that nature He is exalted to be Lord of all. God the Father exalted Jesus because He had humbled Himself, and God crowned Him with glory and honor, the glory which Jesus had before the worlds were.

"Ain't it sweet just to know" that Jesus became a part of us in order to make us become a part of Him? So, if anybody asks you who I am, tell them that I am redeemed, bought with a price. Jesus has changed my whole life. Tell them that I am a child of God; that's who I am!

TALENT FOR GOD

Matthew 25:15-21

Key Verse: Matthew 25:21 - *His lord said unto him, Well done, good and faithful servant: you have been faithful over a few things, I will make you ruler over many things: enter into the joy of your lord.*

The *World Book Dictionary* says that the word "talent" means a special natural ability, an ancient unit of weight or money, varying with time and place. In the theme scripture, which is found in Matthew 25:21, we find the parable of the talents. This parable of the talent is using financial investments as an illustration. These illustrations teach us that we will be held responsible for all of our endowments and opportunities. This includes the use of our gifts, whether one, two, or five.

When I first looked at the word "talent", I immediately thought of the word gift. We might ask, "What is a gift? How are gifts related to talents?" Sometimes we use the terms gifted or talented interchangeably. Strong similarities exist between the talent and the gift, but they are not the same. To compare:

A talent is present from natural birth, / A gift is present from spiritual birth,

Operates through common grace in society, /Operates through special grace in the church,

Communicates any subject, and / Communicates Biblical truth, and

Often yields only understanding of a topic. / Prepares for involvement and obedience.

Now, in the story of the talents, we find the talents being used as a financial investment committed to three servants. The Master is Christ; the servants are Christians. We have three things in general in this parable:

1. We should notice the trust that is committed to these servants. Their master delivered to them his goods, appointed them to work (Christ keeps no servants just to be idle.), and he left them something to work upon. The occasion for this trust to these servants was that the master was traveling unto a far country; what was committed were talents.

2. The different management styles and improvement methods of this trust should be noticed. In verses 16-18 two of the servants did well. They were diligent and faithful; they went and traded. They set about the work immediately and were successful. The third servant did nothing. Verse 18 says that he went and hid his lord's money.

3. The account or responsibility required of the servants should be noticed. In verse 19 the accounting is deferred. It is not until a long time had passed that they were reckoned with, yet the day of accountancy comes at last. The lord of those servants reckoned with them.

We must all give an account of our stewardship, what good we have done for our own souls and what good we have done to/for others. In the story two of the servants acknowledged with thankfulness the master's vouchsafements given to them by saying, "Lord, you delivered to me . . ." It is good to remember what we have received that we may know what is expected from us and may render according to the benefits we will receive. In Psalm 68:9 David said, "Blessed be the Lord, who daily loads us with benefits, even the God of our salvation." He asked in 116:12, "What shall I render unto the Lord for all his benefits toward me?"

My friends, all of us here today have something that God has given us to be used preferably for His glory and for His honor. Whether you are saved or unsaved, Romans 11:29 tells us, "For the gifts and calling of God are without repentance." So, how you choose to use or invest your talent is up to you. God rains on the just and the unjust. God does not change his mind about whom He chooses to bless. Isaiah 46:9-10 tells us, "Remember the former things of old; for I am God, and there is none else; I am God, and there is none else like me, Declaring the end from the beginning, and from ancient times the things that are not yet done, saying, my counsel shall stand, and I will do all my pleasures."

I say unto you today to continue to use your talent for God because accounting day is going to come, and, as the theme scripture stated, if you have been faithful, he will say unto you, "Well done, good and faithful servant; you have been faithful over a few things, I will make you ruler over many things. Enter into the joy of your lord." But, if we are like the lazy servant who hid what the master gave him to work with, He will say, "Take that what I gave to him and give to the faithful. For unto everyone that has shall be given, and he shall have abundance; but from him that have not shall be taken away even that which he has, and cast the unprofitable servant into outer darkness; where there shall be weeping and gnashing of teeth." So, I close by saying that you should use your talent and gift, or else! This is to the young as well as all others. I don't know who wrote this, but I leave this for you to think on:

There's a clever young fellow named Somebody Else--
There's nothing this fellow can't do.
He's busy from morning 'til way late at night
Just substituting for you.

When asked to do this or asked to do that
So often you're set to reply:
"Get Somebody Else, Mr. Chairman,
He'll do it better than I."

There's so much to do in our parish:
So much, and the workers are few.
And Somebody Else gets weary and worn
Just substituting for you.

So, next time you're asked to do something worthwhile
Come up with this honest reply:
"If Somebody Else can give time and support,
It's obviously true, so can I." (Anonymous) Thank you.

KEY OF KNOWLEDGE

Various Scriptures

The *World Book Encyclopedia Dictionary* says that the word "knowledge" applies to all that one knows and understands of facts, general truths and principles whether gained from books and teachers or by personal experience and observation. In the study of *The Principles of Biblical Hermeneutics* by J. Edwin Hartill, we find what is called "The First Mention Principle." The definition is given as, "That principle by which God indicates in the first mention of a subject the truth with which that subject stands connected in the mind of God." Thus, the first time a thing is mentioned in Scripture it carries with it a meaning that will be carried all throughout the Word of God. So, we find the word "knowledge" or a reasonable facsimile (exact copy) all through the Bible.

The first mention is found in Genesis 1:28 which reads, "And God said unto them, be fruitful, and multiply and fill the earth, and subdue it; and have dominion over the fowl of the air, and over every living thing that moves upon the earth." Here we find that man began with a mind in its finite capacity that was for learning, but he did not begin knowing all of the secrets of the universe. Here man is given the divine Magna Charta, a guarantee of rights and privileges, for all true scientific and material progress. He is commanded to subdue, that is to acquire a knowledge and mastery over his material environment in order to bring its elements into the service of the race. This command was given before the fall of man. Before the fall, man was placed in sovereignty over the earth (vs. 28-30), crowned with glory and honor (Psalm 8:5-8), yet subject to God, his creator (Gen. 2:15-17). The divine intention was and is that man should have fellowship with God in obedience. Sin, the essence of which is rebellion against the will of God, came, and man became separated from God (3:17-19). In spite of man's disobedience God still wanted man to have knowledge of Him and the goal that He had to restore sinning man to God's likeness, to fellowship, and to dominion (Romans 8:29; Revelation 21:3; 20:6; 22:5).

Man learned early, by personal experience, that he needed God, and, as stated in Genesis 4:26, "[. . .] then began man to call upon the name of the Lord." We find that knowledge of God is given by God. Psalms 94:10 says, "He who chastises the nations shall not he correct? He who teaches man knowledge, shall he not know?" Proverbs 2:6 says, "For the Lord gives wisdom; out of his mouth come knowledge and understanding." I Corinthians 2:12 states, "Now we have received, not the spirit of the world, but the Spirit who is of God, that we might know the things that are freely given to us of God." Not only does God give us knowledge of Him, but blessings are the results of knowing God. Psalm 89:15 says, "Blessed are the people that know the joyful sound; they shall walk, O Lord, in the light of your countenance."

Just as there are blessings and responsibilities in the knowledge of God, there is danger of the want of God or ignorance of God. Hosea 4:6 says, "My people are destroyed for lack of knowledge; because you have rejected knowledge, I will also reject you." Jeremiah 4:22 tells us, "For my people are foolish, they have not known me; they are silly children, and they have no understanding; they are wise to do evil, but to do good they have no knowledge." I Corinthians 15:34 admonishes us, "Awake to righteousness, and sin not; for some have not the knowledge of God." Brothers and sisters, knowledge can be prayed for and sought after. In John 17:3 Jesus prayed, "And this is life eternal, that they might know you, the only true God, and Jesus Christ whom you have sent." II Peter 1:5 says, "And beside this, giving all diligence, add to your faith virtue, and to virtue knowledge."

Let us not forget that knowledge may be perverted and thus may become the medium of evil. Isaiah 47:10 tells us, "For you have trusted in your wickedness; you have said, none sees me. Your wisdom and your knowledge, it has perverted you; and you have said in your heart, I am, and none else beside me." Let us remember to cherish knowledge. John 10:27 tells us, "My sheep hear my voice, and I know them, and they follow me."

Let us experience knowledge as advised in Ephesians 3:19, "And to know the love of Christ which passes knowledge that you might be filled with all the fullness of God."

Finally, respect divine knowledge; the omniscience of God is the divine attribute of perfect knowledge. We know in part, but God is all knowledge. Proverbs 15:3 lets us know, "The eyes of the Lord are in every place beholding the evil and the good." Isaiah 46:10 adds, "Declaring the end from the beginning, and from ancient times the things that are not yet done, saying, my counsel shall stand, and I will do all my pleasure." Saints, let us, "Study (to know) to show yourself approved unto God, a workman that needs not to be ashamed, rightly diving the word of truth" (II Timothy 2:15). Thank you.

HARVEST HOMECOMING CELEBRATION

Song of Solomon 2:11-13

Song of Solomon 2:11-13 - *For, lo, the winter is past, the rain is over and gone; The flowers appear on the earth; the time of the singing birds is come, and the voice of the turtle is heard in our land; The fig tree puts forth her green figs, and the vines with the tender grape give a good smell [. . .].*

Tonight we are climaxing our Harvest Homecoming Celebration. Tonight I would like to do a mural painting, not on a wall, but in your minds. In the natural sense harvest is the season for gathering in agricultural crops. You might know how this is done if you have ever lived on a farm or have done what some call city farming. This is when you live in the city and raise your own gardens like it is done on a farm. We are not speaking about the natural side although Jesus often used the natural to teach us about the spiritual. In the 15th chapter of John, which is about the vine and the branches, Jesus declared, "I am the vine; you are the branches."

In the Song of Solomon 2:11-13 we find, "For, lo, the winter is past, the rain is over and gone, the flowers appear on the earth; the time of the singing of birds has come, and the voice of the turtledove is heard in our land, the fig tree puts forth her green figs, and the vines with the tender grapes give forth fragrance. [. . .]." Our theme scripture gives a picture of the season: the winter is past, the rain is over and gone, and it's time to get your crops ready for cultivation, no cultivation means no harvest.

Matthew 20:1-16 tells the parable of the laborers who do the cultivating. In this parable the laborers were hired to harvest the crop, to work in the vineyard for "whatever is right." Good workers are hard to find, and sometimes there is a shortage. Matthew 9:36-38 records, "When Jesus saw the multitudes he was moved with compassion and He said, the harvest truly is plenteous but the laborers are few. Pray you, therefore, the Lord of the harvest, that He will send forth laborers into his harvest." Jesus is speaking of a spiritual harvest.

All of these sayings are good and very good, but how does this spiritual reality come about? In this harvest we are mainly dealing with two words: laborers and harvest. In order to have a harvest, we must have laborers. In order to get into the Spiritual labor forces, we are hired by God; that is, He saves us. It is not because we are so good, for Romans 3:10-11 says, "There is none righteous, no, not one: there is none that understands; there is none that seeks after God." Yet, God, in His infinite mercy saves us and sends us forth into His vineyard to work. I want you to remember that when the Bible speaks of a vineyard, it usually has reference to a grape vineyard. Jesus emphatically declared that He was the vine; we are the branches; the grapes are the produce from the branches. So, it is God's vineyard, Jesus is the vine, we are the branches, and thus, we are the laborers.

In the natural sense, when we are hired on a job, the first thing we want to know is about the pay. Then we want to know about the benefits. Now, this is good; it shows that we are concerned about our physical welfare. Why not be more concerned about the spiritual welfare? Now, as spiritual laborers in God's vineyard, our pay is "whatever is right;" we have to trust God. Our benefits are so numerous that David asked, "What shall I render unto the Lord for all His benefits toward me? (Psalms 116:12). Psalms 68:19 says, "Blessed be the Lord, who daily loads us with benefits." In order to fully reap the benefits and efficiently bring in the harvest, we must, "[. . .] lay aside every weight and the sin which does so easily beset us" (Hebrews 12:1).

The harvest does not include unbelievers. We even have some that try to imitate a true laborer, but God's laborers cannot be duplicated. God tells us to do a good work, and when the harvest comes, He will do the separating. To those of us who are in the "I-don't-do-that" group or the "I-can't-go-there" group, we might be mistaken for one of these imitators because we are surrounded by them. We should be careful that some of their misdeeds don't rub off on us. Be thankful that God can tell the difference. We are all sinners saved by Grace, and God is able to save to the uttermost all that come to Him.

We must remember, too, that while we are laboring in the vineyard trying to harvest in some lost soul, we ourselves are going to be tried by fire. We are told not to think it strange because all of God's children will be tried. In Matthew 3:11 John the Baptist tells us, "I, indeed, baptize you with water unto repentance, but he who comes after me is mightier than I, whose shoes I am not worthy to bear; he shall baptize you with the Holy Ghost, and with fire." When God tries us, if we flunk the test, He will give it to us again so that we will not be destroyed. And, finally, in the great harvest all the grapes that were left in the vineyard will be gathered by the angels of God and put into the winepress of God's wrath. So, it behooves us to be real, true laborers for the Lord. Thank you.

CHRISTIAN EDUCATION
AND THE GOSPEL

II Timothy 2:15

II Timothy 2:15 - *Study to show yourself approved unto God, a workman that needs not to be ashamed, rightly dividing the word of truth.*

The theme for this program is "Christian Education and the Gospel" found in II Timothy. The apostle Paul has been credited with being the writer from which the scripture was taken. It was the second epistle of Paul to Timothy. Timothy was born in Lystra; he was child of a mixed marriage--his father was Greek, his mother was a Jewess (Acts 16:1). From early childhood he received religious instruction from his mother Eunice and his grandmother Lois (II Tim.1:5; 3:15). He was converted under Paul's ministry and was set apart for his work by the laying on of hands (I Tim. 4:14).

Timothy became Paul's traveling companion and assistant. At the time of this writing, Paul was in prison, but this did not discourage him. In II Timothy 2:15 he is telling Timothy, "Study to show yourself approved unto God, a workman that needs not to be ashamed, rightly dividing the word of truth." My friends, this challenge is to us today. Have we become learned or educated in the ways of the Lord, or are we still ignorant?

Yes, God wants us to learn of Him. Deuteronomy 6:4-7 tells us, "Hear, O Israel: the Lord our God is one Lord: And you shall love the Lord your God with all your heart, and with all your soul, and with all your might. And these words, which I command you this day, shall be in your heart. And you shall teach them diligently unto your children, and shall talk of them when you sit in your house, and when you walk by the way, and when you lie down, and when you rise up." Proverbs 1:5 says, "A wise man will hear, and will increase learning." Verse 9:9 says, "Give instruction to a wise man, and he will be yet wiser: teach a just man, and he will increase in learning." Psalm 25:4-5 pleads, "Show me your ways O Lord; teach me your paths. Lead me in your truth and teach me." In Matthew 11:29 Jesus said, "Take my yoke upon you and learn of me." My friends, God wants us to know about him, to teach about him, and "In all of your ways acknowledge him, and he shall direct your paths" (Proverbs 3:6).

Now, let us take a good look at many of our churches of today. Our Sunday School has fallen away attendance wise. The mid-week prayer service does well to have a few die-hard saints in attendance if we still have one. The training union has died a thousand deaths. I say unto you, my sisters and brothers, without any doubt at all, if Christian men and women are to grow in grace and in the knowledge of the Lord and Savior Jesus Christ and if children and youth are to increase in wisdom and stature and in favor of God and man like the boy Jesus, the church must take seriously the teaching ministry. If the teaching ministry is to make its mark upon the church, the matter of leadership education is vital and crucial.

Each member of the church should know what the Scripture says our duties toward God are. First of all, we should attend Bible school and training union weekly or as often as available. Again, II Timothy 2:15 say, "Study to show yourself approved unto God, a workman that needs not to be ashamed, rightly dividing the word of truth." Secondly, we should attend morning and evening worship every Sunday. Hebrews 10:25 tells us, "Not forsaking the assembling of ourselves together, as the manner of some is; but exhorting one another; and so much more as you see the day approaching."

Next, we should attend mid-week prayer service if available. Ephesians 5:19:20 says, "Speaking to yourselves in psalms and hymns and spiritual songs, singing and making melody in your heart to the Lord." Then, we should partake of the Lord's Supper. I Corinthians 11:26 tells us, "For as often as you eat this bread and drink this cup, you do show the Lord's death till he come."

Another thing is that we should give. In the Old Testament the law required a worshipper to give one-tenth of his income in whatever form it might be; this was called the tithe which is where giving to God starts. There were also many offerings, including a free-will offering (Leviticus 22:18). Since the law of the Old Testament is our schoolmaster (Galatians 3:24), the tithe is a good guideline in determining what is right when you want to give as God has blessed you. God teaches us in the New Testament that all we have belongs to Him. We do not give to him; we only hand over what belongs to him. We are stewards who manage and control God's property for him. One day we must render an account. Therefore, contribute regularly and systematically as God has blessed. I Corinthians 16:2 says, "Upon the first day of the week let every one of you lay by him in store, as God has prospered him, that there be no gatherings when I come."

We should also remember that upon removal from one place to another we should as soon as possible unite with some other church as emphasized in the Church Covenant. Acts 9: 26, 28 tells us, "And when Saul was come to Jerusalem, he assayed to join himself to the disciples; [. .] And he was with them coming in and going out at Jerusalem." Finally, my friends, our earnest and sincere desire each day should be:

- Begin the day with God - pray.
- Open the book of God - study.
- Go through the day with God at work, home, or abroad - abide
- Converse in mind with God - meditate.
- Conclude the day with God - confess.
- Lie down at night with God - rest.

Thank you.

SUGGESTED TOPICS TO BE DEVELOPED

A. **PICKED OUT TO BE PICKED ON**

   1. Moses - Exodus 3:1-10

   2. Elijah - I Kings 17:1; 18:17-40

   3. Jesus - Matthew 1:21; Hebrews 10:5-7

B. **GOD USES ORDINARY PEOPLE TO DO EXTRAORDINARY THINGS**

   1. Peter - Matthew 10:1-2, 5

   2. Paul - Acts 9:13-16

   3. John - Luke 1:57, 66

The three can be used on one program with three different speakers or may be developed individually or used together in a sermon, theme-based address, etc.

B. **NO BURN OUT, ONLY SUCCESS**

Joshua 1:7-9

BIBLIOGRAPHY

Davis, John J. *Biblical Numerology: A Basic Study of the Use of Numbers in the Bible.* Baker Book House. Grand Rapids, Michigan, 1968.

Good News Bible: The Bible in Today's English Version. American Bible Society. New York, 1976.

Halley's Bible Handbook: New Revised Edition. Zondervan Publishing House. Grand Rapids, Michigan, 24th Edition, 1965

Hartill, D.D., J. Edwin. *Principles of Biblical Hermeneutics.* Zondervan Publishing House. Grand Rapids, Michigan, 29th printing, 1980.

Scofield, D. D., Rev. C. I. Ed. *The Scofield Reference Bible: Authorized King James Version.* Oxford University Press. New York, 1945.

Sharp, C. J. *New Training for Service.* Standard Publishing Company. Cincinnati, Ohio, 1934.

Strong, James, S.T.D., LL.D. *The Exhaustive Concordance of the Bible.* Holman Bible Publishers. Nashville, Tennessee, 1992

Unger, Th. D., Ph.D., Merrell F. *Unger's Bible Handbook.* Moody Press. Chicago, 1967.

Webster's Seventh New Collegiate Dictionary. G & C Merriam Company Publishers. Springfield, Massachusetts, 1967.

SEEDS FOR SERMONS TALKS, & ADDRESSES:
Theme-based papers done and compiled by **Mary L. Hampton Battle**
Edited and submitted by her daughter, **EDNA YVONNE JAMES**

ABOUT THE AUTHOR
Mary Lee Hampton Battle was born in Zama, Mississippi, but reared in Greenville, Mississippi. She accepted Christ as her personal Savior at the age of twelve and was baptized at St. Paul Church in Greenville. Mary graduated Salutatorian of Coleman High School in Greenville where she received a Provisional Certificate and became a school teacher right out of high school. Due to her mother's illness, Mary decided to forego college and attend to her mother. Not able to renew her certificate, she had to find other resources.

After her mother's illness was stabilized and recovery was ensuing, Mary relocated in the East St. Louis, Illinois, area where her parents soon joined her. She always lived near her mother and father and was able to continue attending to her mother's health issue. Mary and her family resided mostly in Centreville, Illinois, where she united with Calvary Missionary Baptist Church. At Calvary, God stirred up the gift of teaching. Mary was a Sunday School, Monday Night Bible Study, Wednesday night Mission, Vacation Bible School, and Bible Study Workshop teacher. She further honed her skills by attending Brooks Bible Institute.

Calvary affiliated with the New Zion District Association of the Illinois Baptist State Convention, Incorporated, where Mary was elected as the local President of the Women's Auxiliary and served from 1974 until 1997. Each year the district would select a theme for its annual session. These themes fielded The President's Annual Addresses of twenty-three years that make up the bulk of this book, *Seeds for Sermons, Talks, and Addresses*. Mary also taught in the district's Annual Christian Education Session.

Over the years Mary L. Hampton Battle was not only known for her teaching skills but was also known for her oratorical skills. She was often invited to speak at many Women's Day services and other occasions because her talks were always Bible-based, very educational, and very spiritual for she only gave out what the Lord gave her. Mary was also a skilled seamstress and tailor. Mary taught, spoke, and sewed until her health failed. Mary's journey here on earth ended, and God took her home on September 8, 2003.

ABOUT THE EDITOR

Edna Yvonne James is the third child of Mary L. Hampton Battle. The other siblings are James (deceased), and Joseph Harris, Kay Morris, Evelyn Clay, and John Charles Hampton (deceased). Edna followed in her mother's footsteps of teaching; Edna, like her mother has the gift of teaching. After graduating from Lincoln Senior High School in East St. Louis, Illinois, Edna attended Southern Illinois University in Edwardsville, Illinois, where she obtained a Bachelor of Science in Secondary Education, a Master of Arts in English Language and Literature, and her Administrative Certification. Her mother, Mary L. Hampton Battle, was adamant about her finishing college after she learned that Edna had decided to get married to Harvey Leonard James before graduating from college. Edna and Harvey have three children: Terrell, David, and De Andre' James.

Not only did Edna teach secularly but God also stirred up the gift of teaching at Calvary Missionary Baptist Church where she had united and was baptized at the age of twelve. Edna was also a Sunday School, Monday Night Bible Study, Wednesday night Mission, Vacation Bible School, and Bible Study Workshop teacher. Edna established the Calvary Board of Christian Education and became the Director of Christian Education. Edna admired her mother for her humility and willingness to sit under her daughter's teaching and also to teach under Edna's direction.

Edna also followed in her mother's footstep as she was elected to fulfill the position of President of the Women's Auxiliary of The New Zion District Association of the Illinois Baptist State Convention, Inc., after her mother, Mary Hampton Battle, stepped down to make room for a younger person. Edna also inherited her mother's oratorical skills because she has spoken at several Women's Day services. Edna will continue to serve the Lord until her journey here on earth ends.

CPSIA information can be obtained at www.ICGtesting.com
Printed in the USA
LVOW110312070612

284971LV00003B/1/P